The MEXICAN

HOUSE Old & New

The MEXICAN
HOUSE Old & New

by Verna Cook Shipway and Warren Shipway

ARCHITECTURAL BOOK PUBLISHING CO., INC.

NEW YORK

SECOND PRINTING, JULY 1963

THIRD PRINTING, OCTOBER 1963

FOURTH PRINTING, AUGUST 1964

FIFTH PRINTING, AUGUST 1965

SIXTH PRINTING, AUGUST 1966

SEVENTH PRINTING, OCTOBER 1968

EIGHTH PRINTING, SEPTEMBER 1970

NINTH PRINTING, OCTOBER 1972

Published simultaneously in Canada
by Saunders, of Toronto, Ltd., Don Mills, Ontario

ISBN: 8038-0158-0

Library of Congress Catalog Card Number: 60-14620

Printed in the United States of America

CONTENTS

V

Table of Contents

Mexican architectural heritage is amazingly rich and many layered. A wealth of varied influences, with Moorish-Arabic spicing those of European descent, left their imaginative imprints upon the art of Spain. In Mexico, during the early years following the Spanish Conquest, these influences were subordinated to the need for security: structures were massive, readily adaptable for defense. Later, however, the native Indians, descendants of the great builders and sculptors of pre-Conquest centuries, were given latitude in their execution of the decorative schemes brought from Spain by clerical and lay architects. It was this combination which produced the vitality of the heritage which Mexico possesses today.

Traditional motifs and bits and pieces of Colonial design are shown on the following pages by photographs and a number of measured drawings. Some are from homes constructed during the 17th and 18th centuries, some from remodeled houses, and many from those built within the past twenty years. Each shows in its way the continuance of the virile strain of a regal era of grace and elegance.

Today, as you laze along a street in an urban area, except for an occasional vine, luxurious in color, creeping over a linking wall, no greenery softens the severe expanse of plain façades. The colors of these usually plastered and water-painted walls are too subtle for accurate description. Bleached under a brilliant sun and weathered by tempestuous summer rains, they have become multi-hued. They are said to be the despair of painters.

Here and there and only where necessary, are openings — windows protectively grilled with wrought iron and, always, a noteworthy entrance doorway. The latter, at times, is framed by a decorative surround in stone or plaster, but more often it is merely set into a rectangular wall piercing. Whether simple or embellished, the door itself is a heavy one, either patterned with moulded panels or else handsomely iron-studded.

A glimpse through such a doorway is an adventure. Beyond the cool shade of the *zaguan* or entryway is the brilliance of a patio with its murmuring fountain surrounded by a profusion of flowering vine and potted bloom. It is within these enchanted areas that many of the following pictures were taken.

We wish to thank all of those who through their courtesy made possible for us the carrying out of our enjoyable undertaking. And it was solely owing to their helpfulness that we are now able to greet you, as you open this book, with an extension of their gracious welcome, "*Ésta es su casa,*" "This is your house."

List of Houses

List of Houses

Pase usted, por favor. Ésta es su casa.

Apaseo el Grande, Guanajuato

Down an unsuspected byway stands this glory of the baroque, formerly known as the Casa de los Condes de la Cadena, constructed in 1789 by masons brought from Spain and France.
Farmyard adjoining rear of mansion. Scrolled work is molded in plaster over corbeled brick.

Apaseo el Grande, Guanajuato

(Above) Now a seminary, but formerly the private home of the Urquiza family. Designed in the early years of the 19th century by a noted artist and architect of the Mexican colonial period, Francisco Eduardo de Tresguerras.

(Right) Wrought-iron railing at central arch of *galería,* seen from inside.

Pátzcuaro, Michoacán

Casa de los Escudos, or House of the Shields, an 18th-century residence then belonging to the Solorzano family. Its *portales* provide a covered walk along the Plaza Grande, with columns and arches of stone supporting adobe walls. Narrow bands of molded brick swing from stone-trimmed windows to carved stone shields.

Taxco, Guerrero

(Above) The façade of this house has many decorative ecclesiastical details. It was built by José de la Borda for his son, who was the first priest, 1759 to 1775, of the famous Taxco church dedicated to San Sebastián and Santa Prisca.

(Left) The over-all raised ornamentation, cut from the plaster, is painted pink over yellow, harmonizing with the greyed-pink stone of windows and entrance door.

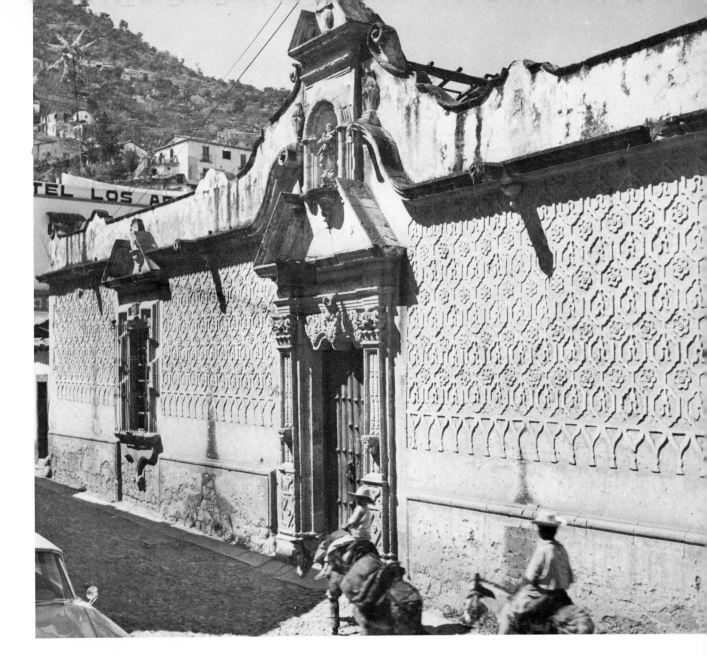

Taxco, Guerrero

(Above) Casa de Villanueva, dating from the 18th century, is now known as Casa Humboldt because the renowned engineer, Baron Alexander von Humboldt, stayed here briefly during his Mexican travels. Of *barroco-mudéjar* style, it contrasts strikingly the fancies of major baroque features against a richly patterned wall of Moorish motifs.

(Left) The cast-brass knocker of the door above.

Taxco, Guerrero

An old house on the Plaza del Ex-Convento with wide overhanging eave protecting the balcony and sawn-wood balustrade below. Diagonal braces support the heavy load of the tile on the frail rafters. Plastered adobe walls are painted white with dark red bands outlining doors and windows; woodwork is painted greyed bottle green.

PHOTOGRAPH BY HUGO BREHME

Taxco, Guerrero

A most picturesque colonial town built on a steep mountainside, with narrow cobblestone streets. As is customary in such communities, the rough adobe walls are plastered to protect the mud and straw blocks from the ravages of violent rains. Painted and repainted year after year in soft shades of various colors, the result is one of great charm. With roofs of weathered red tile, and lacelike parapets and balconies, these quaint little houses nestle against each other as they climb the slope.

Valenciana, Guanajuato

The least like that of a miner and the most elegant home in or about Guanajuato was that of the Conde Rul, grandee of the silver lords. Evident is the influence of the Moors in the simple expanse of plain wall surfaces, broken only where functionally necessary by imposing carved stone openings. The rubble masonry walls are plastered and painted a greyed cream rose, approaching the color of the cut-stone trim of door and windows.

Oaxaca, Oaxaca

A *casa baja,* or one-story house, of massive construction for earthquake resistance,
enhanced by the restrained ornamental grace of a curved pedimented doorway.

Pátzcuaro, Michoacán

Unique are the *portales* on the Plaza de la Parroquía del Carmen. Squared and rounded wood columns support the second floor with its customary wood balconies and *barandal* of turned wood balusters. Octagonal wood pillars carry the ceiling of the porch, or *corredor superior,* above, all under a roof of red-brown tile.

Santa Clara del Cobre, Michoacán

The abundance of lumber on the rolling hills around Lake Pátzcuaro made possible a wide use of slender wood columns with naïvely designed Ionic wood capitals and *zapatas*, or pillow blocks, above. These support the heavy girders which carry the ceiling beams and rafters.

Pátzcuaro, Michoacán

A typical street scene. The shaped-end ceiling beams of these one-story houses, projecting beyond the exterior walls, carry the rafters and also provide weather protection for the narrow sidewalks. The white-plastered adobe walls have painted dados, usually of dark red, with painted eave soffits above.

PHOTOGRAPH BY GUILLERMO ZAMORA

(Above) *Cuernavaca, Morelos*

This house is new in simplicity of design and in the use of glass walls for maximum admission of light. Yet it retains many traditional elements of colonial days, such as the tiled roof, the hooded fireplace, and the native type of rubblework.

(Left) *Apaseo el Grande, Guanajuato*

Elegant in design is the stone chimney top over the masonry hood seen through the glass; the same chimney is shown on page 140.

Cuernavaca, Morelos

A stone-trimmed *galería*, traditionally colonial, forms an open-walled room as the main approach to the *sala* of this recently designed home.

Favored symbolic motifs carved in stone — the shell and the Aztec sun made into a face — are decoratively set between the arch swings.

Cuernavaca, Morelos

The designer of this newly built clubhouse, markedly imbued with the spirit and tradition of Mexico's colonial architecture, has cleverly used water, both in pools and fountains, to blend landscaping and structure. The reflection of the white façade, with its arcade outlined in cut stone, gives added importance by a seeming increase in scale.

(Above) *Marfil, Guanajuato*

The partially reconstructed wall of a former silver-ore-reduction hacienda, characteristic because of its projecting roof spouts and its hooded window openings with carved-stone-corbeled sills and *rejas*, or wrought-iron grilles.

(Left) *Oaxaca, Oaxaca*

A detail of an earlier *reja*, with motifs similar to those above.

(Above) *Guanajuato, Guanajuato*

The wealth of varied influences which prevailed in Europe during the Mexican colonial period have left their indelible stamps. Of marked kinship to the studied formality of the late Georgian style in England is this house on the Paseo de la Presa.

(Left) *Morelia, Michoacán*

A familiar door knocker of cast brass. The frilly cuff and ring on the finger are characteristic.

(Above) *San Miguel de Allende, Guanajuato*

An open *corredor* forming one side of a sun-splashed patio. Time has mellowed to earthy colors these gaily swinging arches, creating a foil for the vivid coloring of flowering vines and potted blooms. Cerise, magenta, tangerine, and pale blue-green mixed at random seem to belong under a brilliant sun.

(Right) *Pátzcuaro, Michoacán*

Imaginative native treatment of a carved keystone.

18

Cuernavaca, Morelos

Corredores and *galerías* fronting on patios are usually faced south, in the warmer regions, to take advantage of the climate, delightful the year around, and yet avoid the hot afternoon sun. Sturdily built and spacious, they are definitely exterior in character, but furnished as an interior room, since it is here that the day's living is enjoyed.

That captivating color, "Mexican pink," warmly contrasts against the cool, deep shadows of this *galería* — an elusive color, defying description. Perhaps it is a simple yellowish pink, or perhaps a medley of subtle pinks — the pinks of azaleas, of hibiscus, of wild roses — but bleached from sunshine and water-streaked to reveal underlying hues of mauves and umbers.

Taxco, Guerrero

(Above) The rear loggia of Casa de Villanueva overlooks a deep *barranca* with a
superb panorama through the arches, on
the opposite page, of the mountains to
the east.

The doorway above, carved from greyish
pink stone, combines ecclesiastical motifs
in its keyblock with Moorish-inspired de-
signs of its head and pilasters.

(Right) Stone corbels terminate the four-
arch swing.

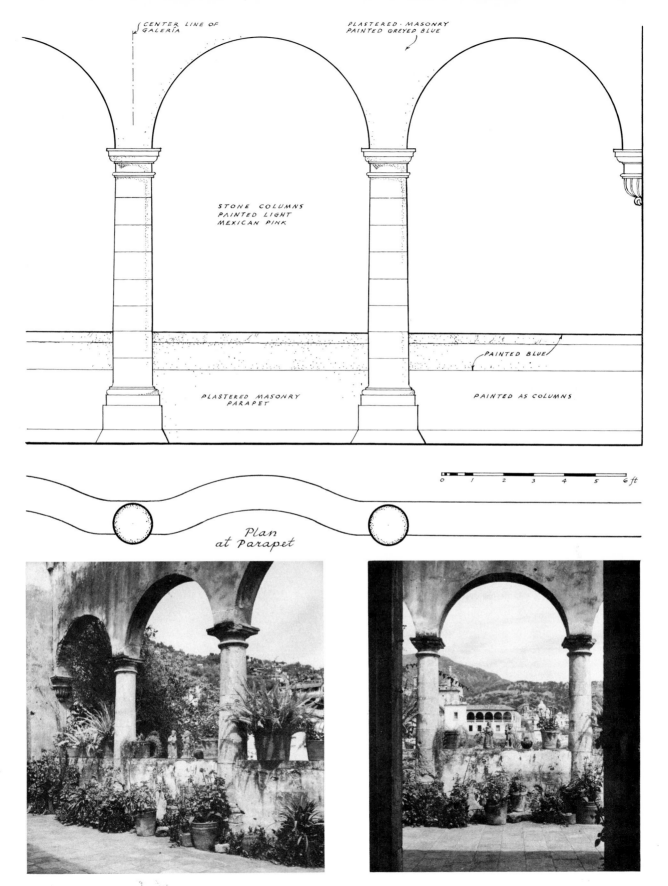

CENTER LINE OF
GALERÍA

PLASTERED·MASONRY
PAINTED GREYED BLUE

STONE COLUMNS
PAINTED LIGHT
MEXICAN PINK

PAINTED BLUE

PLASTERED MASONRY
PARAPET

PAINTED AS COLUMNS

0   1   2   3   4   5   6 ft

Plan
at Parapet

Taxco, Guerrero

Open arcades are one of the outstanding
features of old Mexico. Their gracious
form adds to the welcome atmosphere of
cool seclusion.

(Above) at El Atascadero, San Miguel de
Allende, Guanajuato, the masonry wall
mass, unlike the more typical treatment
shown below, is pargeted with white cement. Painted roofing brick, spanning the
hewn beams, carries the white across the
ceiling.

(Right) In Cuernavaca, Morelos, at Casa
de Piedra, the added height of the *galería*
lends a lofty dignity.

Marfil, Guanajuato

(Above) Great entrance doors give onto a patio enclosed by the imposing masonry walls of a former silver-ore-reduction hacienda in the bottom of the deep-cleft Cañon de Marfil. Greenish-grey stone and mortar joints spotted with slivers of the same stone are partially covered with a breathtaking expanse of bougainvillea.

(Left) Exterior platform of entrance above, with a radiant sun composed of pieces of red tile and light-colored flagstone.

(Above) *Marfil, Guanajuato*

The easterly portion of the patio shown on the preceding page, with its carved stone fountain. The arched area to the right of this former hacienda is now a part of the living quarters of this inspiring home.

(Right) *Tlaquepaque, Jalisco*

Stone cistern now in the Museo. Fish are symbolic of life.

Marfil, Guanajuato

A view of the patio on facing page. The massive intermediate arches of grey-green limestone formerly carried the high roof over the central corridor of the hacienda with lower roofs on each side. Vertical stone louvers near the ceiling provided ventilation.

Morelia, Michoacán

The patio of a residence given to Gener-
alísimo Morelos and briefly occupied by
him prior to his capture and death.

(Above) Pink stone columns and trim
form a harmony, high in key, with the
white plastered masonry walls. The unfinished wood girders of the *galería* are
covered on the patio face with painted
sheet metal to protect them from the rains.

(Right) Built in about 1758 when the
curved line became dominant, the sawn
wood girders supporting the *galería* are
graceful details of the domestic architecture of the period.

26

Pátzcuaro, Michoacán

Counterplay of contrasts is inherent in the architecture of Mexico, such as the dark cool of the arcade silhouetted against the intense light of the patio. The succession of Mudéjar-Gothic arches forming this portico are outlined with bands of Mexican pink against the white wall above. The arch soffits, similarly painted pink, blend with the rosy tint of the native stone. Across the patio, slender wood posts, painted a deeper pink, carry shoes and girder of this darker color, topped with a balustrade of geometric Mudéjar patterning.

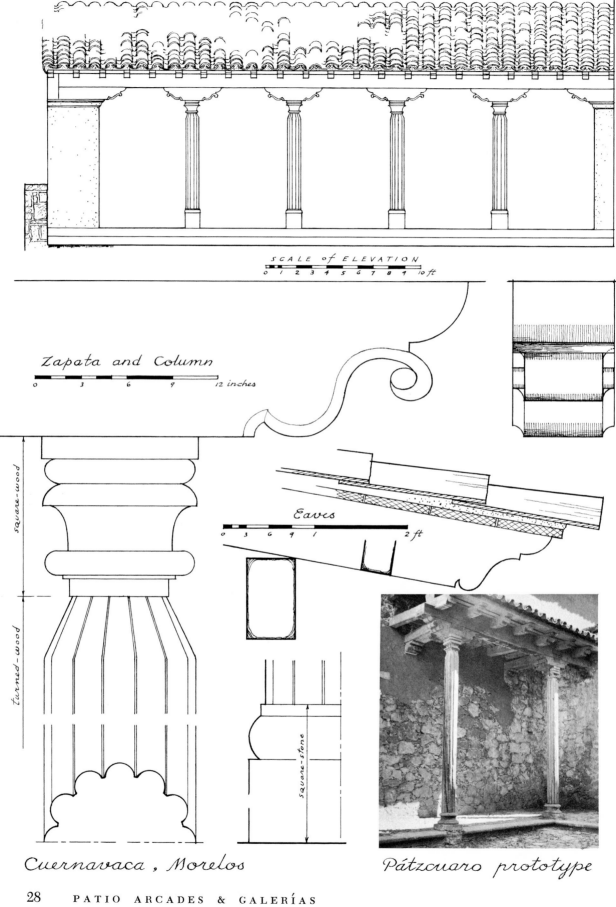

SCALE of ELEVATION

0 1 2 3 4 5 6 7 8 9 10 ft

Zapata and Column

0 3 6 9 12 inches

square-wood

turned-wood

Eaves

0 3 6 9 1 2 ft

square-stone

Cuernavaca, Morelos

Pátzcuaro prototype

Cuernavaca, Morelos

The reeded wood columns, the capitals and *zapatas* of this home under construction
are detailed on the page opposite. They are modeled after the Pátzcuaro prototype.

Pátzcuaro, Michoacán

"Place of Delights," as this quaint town was known to the Tarascan Indians, has changed little in appearance in the last 200 years.

(Above) Secluded inner court with timid, hugged-in volutes on its Ionic capitals.

(Right) Old gallery along the rear patio in the Instituto Nacional de Antropologia e Historia, housed in an old colonial mansion.

(Above) *Querétaro, Querétaro*

Wealth from a fertile valley and nearby mines left this colonial city with many luxurious homes.

Wood *zapatas*, or beam shoes, between columns and the girder above were often fancifully contoured. In many cases the unprotected face of a *zapata* is covered with sheet metal cut to the same outline. Here additional protection for the girders is provided by scalloped metal valances. A happy contrast is gained by the white sheet metal against the rose-pink stone columns.

(Right) *Pátzcuaro, Michoacán*

A *zapata* terminating in two carved consoles with projecting toothlike floor brick above.

31

A colonnade in miniature, bewitchingly outlined in scrolls on quaint posts, was brought from a 200-year-old house in Tinganbato to enrich the folk art at the Instituto Nacional de Antropologia e Historia.

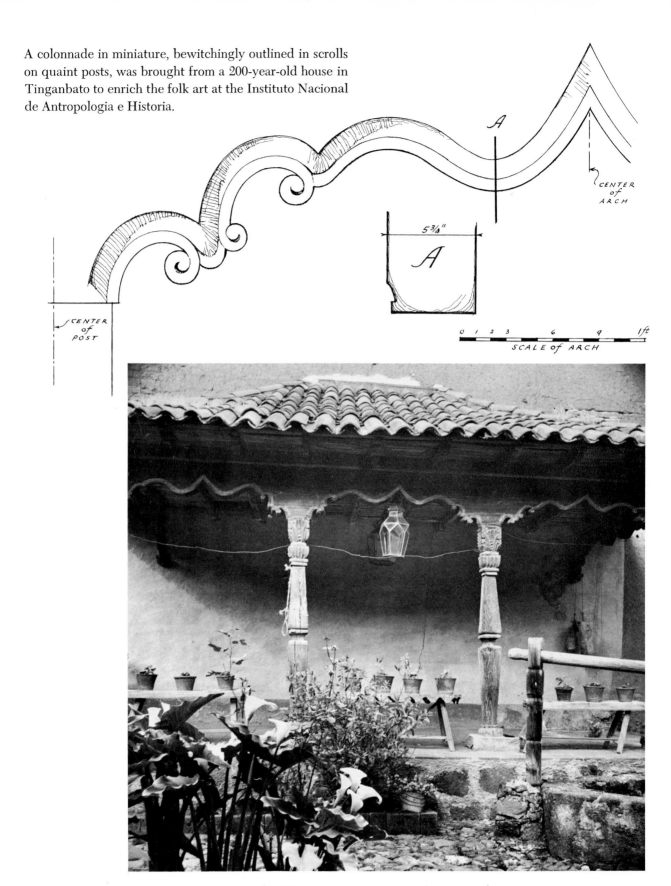

Pátzcuaro , Michoacán

Apaseo el Grande, Guanajuato

With their natural tendency for the ornate, the Spaniards welcomed the Italian baroque, transplanting it to New Spain where it blossomed into a temperamental expression of pomp and joy.

(Above) A patio arch. Barely credible is the magnificent and intricate achievement of the mason maestro and his craftsmen.

(Right) Archway at passage linking patio with farm courtyard.

Querétaro, Querétaro

Patio of a neighboring house of that on the facing page, built in the same years and under the same tamed baroque influence for the Marques de la Villa del Villar del Aquila.

To the wrought-iron railing around the *galería* are attached rings, a customary and practical way of hanging flowerpots.

Querétaro, Querétaro

This town house of the early 18th century follows the Spanish custom of backing upon the street with its beauty displayed around an inner court. Heightening the romanticism and gaiety of the brilliant white arches is the blaze of purple bloom of the bougainvillea vine.

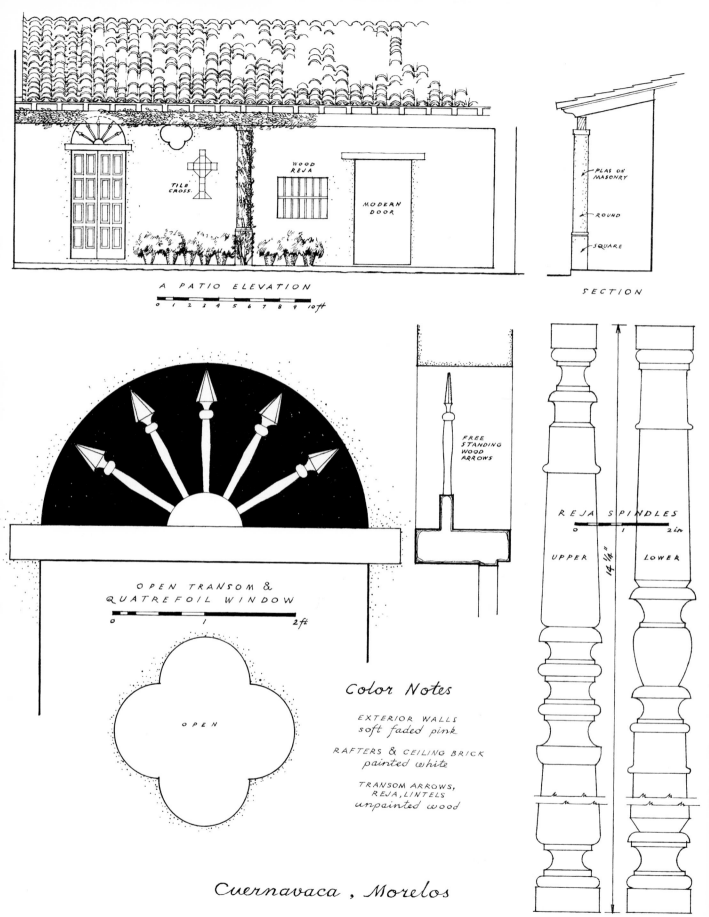

A PATIO ELEVATION

0 1 2 3 4 5 6 7 8 9 10 ft

TILE CROSS.

WOOD REJA

MODERN DOOR

SECTION

PLAS ON MASONRY

ROUND

SQUARE

OPEN TRANSOM & QUATREFOIL WINDOW

0 1 2 ft

OPEN

FREE STANDING WOOD ARROWS

REJA SPINDLES

0 1 2 in

UPPER

LOWER

14 1/4"

Color Notes

EXTERIOR WALLS
soft faded pink

RAFTERS & CEILING BRICK
painted white

TRANSOM ARROWS,
REJA, LINTELS
unpainted wood

Cuernavaca, Morelos

Cuernevaca, Morelos

One of this town's early homes, which escaped destruction during the revolutions.

(Above) Bedroom wing forming one side of the patio.

(Left) The patio and its pool looking toward the *zaguán* on the right and, on the left, the arcade in front of the main *sala*.

Guanajuato, Guanajuato

Birthplace, in 1886, of Diego Rivera. Of particular interest are the peacock-crested scrolls of the braces, the lead ornamentation of the iron balustrade, and the carved stone molding supporting the balcony floor.

(Above) *Puebla, Puebla*

Adorning an austerely plain façade, this *balcon corrido*, or running balcony, and its wrought-iron balustrade with scrolled braces produce a fascinating pattern of shadows in the brilliant Mexican sunshine.

(Left) *San Martin Texmelucan, Puebla*

Of earlier date is the wrought-iron brace forged into a floral design.

(Above) *Querétaro, Querétaro*

Cut stone sections, cantilevered from the wall, form this exterior extension of the second floor. Nineteenth-century iron balustrade with lead ornamentation.

(Right) *Guanajuato, Guanajuato*

Wrought-iron *barandal* edging the *galería* of the patio in the 18th-century Casa de los Condes de Pérez Gálvez.

Querétaro, Querétaro

(Above) By the late 18th century there evolved in Mexico a distinguished combination of wrought iron and masonry. The iron balcony, in general use in Spain in the late 17th century, descended from the stern stone parapet built solely for defense.

    The diagonal bracket of this wrap-around balcony, on pale yellow walls, is intricately carved with pierced C-scrolls from yellow-pink limestone.

(Left) A similar C-scroll pattern is repeated in the wrought-iron railing.

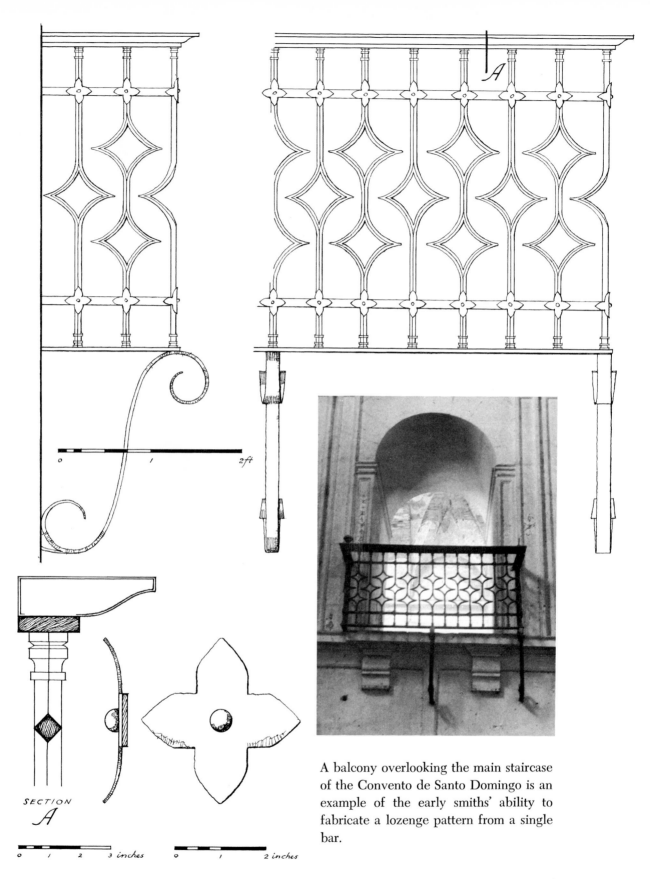

A balcony overlooking the main staircase of the Convento de Santo Domingo is an example of the early smiths' ability to fabricate a lozenge pattern from a single bar.

SECTION
A

0 1 2 3 inches   0 1 2 inches

Oaxaca, Oaxaca

Puebla, Puebla

(Above) A 17th-century *galería*. The floor is of paving brick with glazed-tile inserts. Elegant hand-forged wall braces stiffen the simple wrought-iron balustrade to patio walls of creamy pink.

(Left) The turned brass finials of the railing are repeated atop the braces.

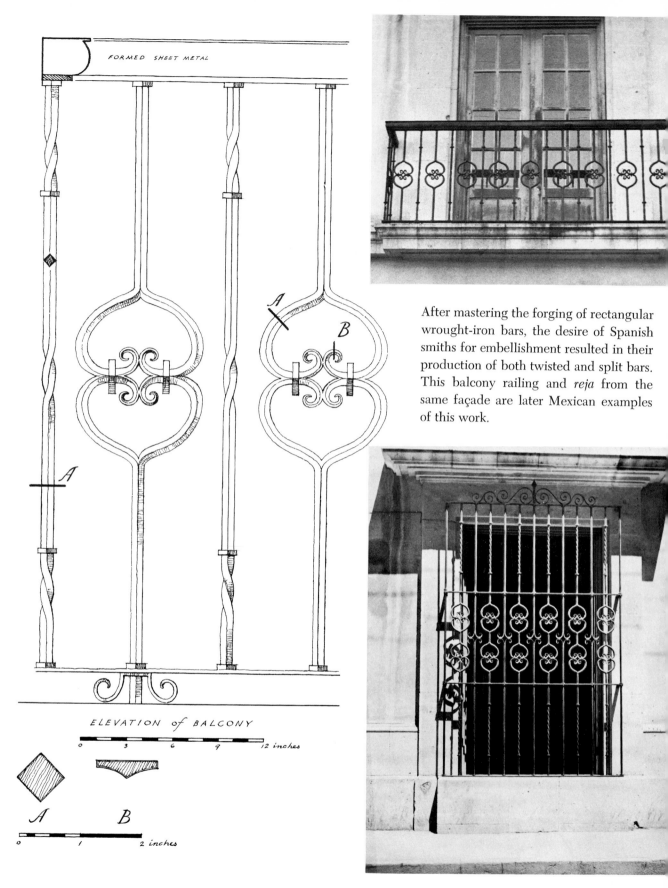

FORMED SHEET METAL

A

B

A

ELEVATION of BALCONY

0   3   6   9   12 inches

A   B

0   1   2 inches

After mastering the forging of rectangular wrought-iron bars, the desire of Spanish smiths for embellishment resulted in their production of both twisted and split bars. This balcony railing and *reja* from the same façade are later Mexican examples of this work.

Oaxaca, Oaxaca

Querétaro, Querétaro

The Old-World atmosphere of Querétaro spreads through street after street.

Pátzcuaro, Michoacán

Typical of the quaint old towns and villages of this region are these narrow balconies with wood balustrades.

(Above) *Banderilla, Vera Cruz*

Near Jalapa, in the giant mountains of the Sierra Madre Range, weaves the main street of this pueblo with its picturesque string of houses. A liberal supply of wood for building material gives a different look to the homes of this tropical region, with their spreading eaves and heavy overhanging balconies.

(Left) *Valle de Guadalupe, Jalisco*

As gracefully proportioned as the broken pedimented top is the reverse curve of the balcony floor projecting over a rope molding and dentil course.

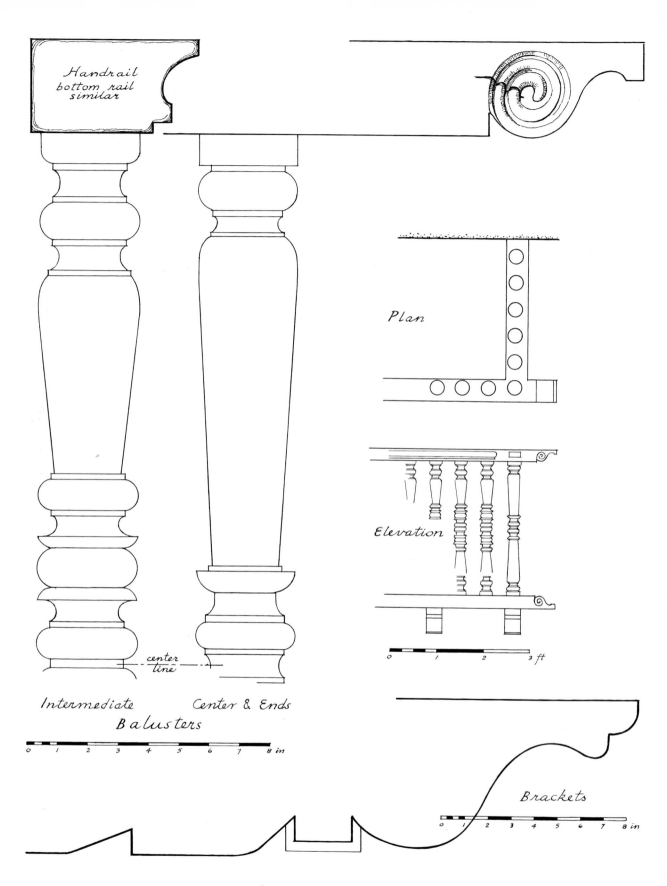

Handrail
bottom rail
similar

Plan

Elevation

0   1   2   3 ft

Intermediate   Center & Ends
Balusters

0 1 2 3 4 5 6 7 8 in

center
line

Brackets

0 1 2 3 4 5 6 7 8 in

Taxco, Guerrero

Taxco, Guerrero

The wooden balcony on the Plaza Mayor is distinctive because of the carved, extended endings of its top and bottom rails and its turned spindles, all detailed on the page opposite.

Pátzcuaro, Michoacán

Slender unpainted wooden spindles, carried upon a much-molded balcony projection of masonry, tie the doorway below into a composition with the French window above and its plaster-modeled headpiece.

Parras de la Fuente, Coahuila

Predominant against a spacious and otherwise unadorned wall are the iron-railed balconies with stone pendants in bold scale. Possibly because of a likeness to banners flung from windows, such hanging features are called curtains, or *cortinas*.

Apaseo el Grande, Guanajuato
Superimposed layers of stone cut to varying outlines, with a sun face climaxing the design, show the skill and taste of Tresguerras.

Guanajuato, Guanajuato
Tasselled valance carved from local green stone in the 18th century.

San Miguel de Allende, Guanajuato
Dramatic effect of swagged draperies shaped in stone.

Apaseo el Grande, Guanajuato
A baroque whimsey, with its New-World acquisition of charm.

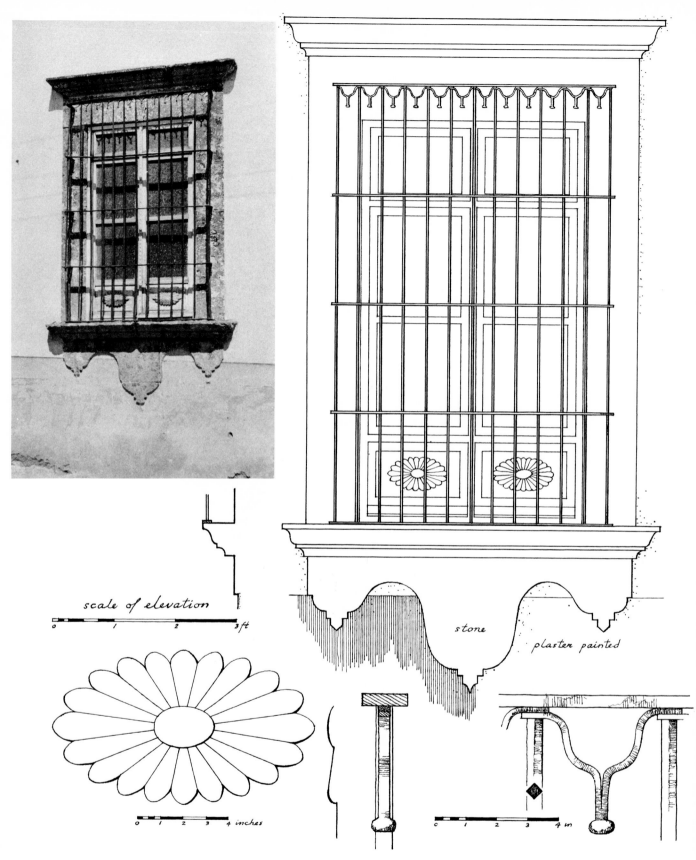

scale of elevation

0   1   2   3 ft

stone

plaster painted

0   1   2   3   4 inches

0   1   2   3   4 in

San Miguel de Allende, Guanajuato

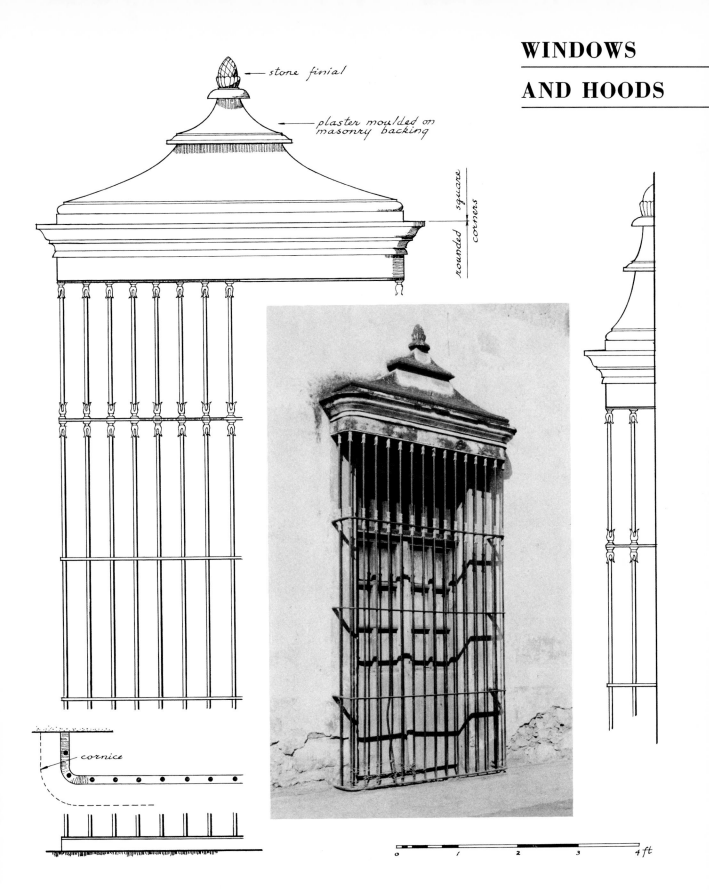

stone finial

plaster moulded on
masonry backing

rounded square corners

cornice

Yautepec, Morelos

Near *Guanajuato, Guanajuato*

A pretentious design, unaffectedly and artlessly executed.

A charmingly simple, upside-down and elongated console projects from a deep-toned pink wall to form a cap for the iron *reja* of a later period.

Cuernavaca, Morelos

(Left) *Cuautla, Morelos*

The quaint peaked cap and curved *reja* give this window the appearance of an openwork bay.

(Right) *Tlacotepec, Puebla*

Rectangular in plan, this hooded top swings upward, pagodalike.

Cuernavaca, Morelos

The aged custom of barring windows with iron for protection was brought to New Spain by the Conquistadores who taught the Indians how to work this metal. The tile eaves overhanging this quaintly guarded second-story window, set into a weathered and water-streaked off-white wall, is painted in a delightful design with tones of peach.

Oaxaca, Oaxaca   Crested 19th-century window grilles with lead ornamentation.

Typical wrought-iron flowers and corner brace and round-bar *reja* of the colonial period.

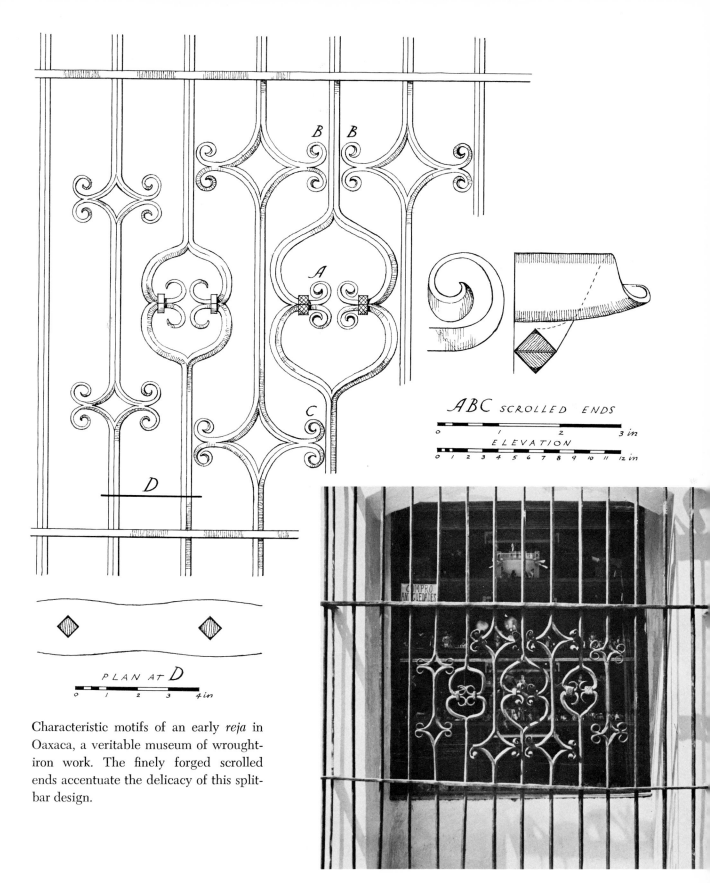

ABC SCROLLED ENDS

0   1   2   3 in

ELEVATION

0 1 2 3 4 5 6 7 8 9 10 11 12 in

PLAN AT *D*

0   1   2   3   4 in

Characteristic motifs of an early *reja* in Oaxaca, a veritable museum of wrought-iron work. The finely forged scrolled ends accentuate the delicacy of this split-bar design.

Oaxaca, Oaxaca

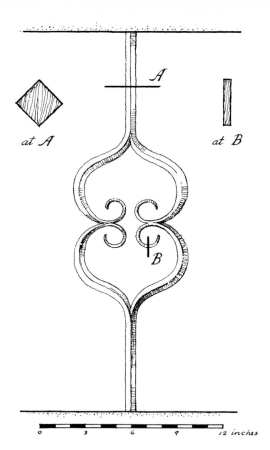

Cuernavaca, Morelos

A typical heart-shaped iron motif protects this small window opening.

Querétaro, Querétaro

One of two balancing windows flanking a side door of the Parroquia de Santiago. The arrows with leaded heads, feathers, and rosette recall the French Empire.

Marfil, Guanajuato

With tasseled head and basic C-scroll, this old wrought-iron grille screens a wall opening.

A window grille fabricated during the mid-18th century for the Conde Rul. Its ornamentation, applied on wrought-iron square bars, is reminiscent of the earlier work of Spanish smiths.

0   3   6   9   1   2 ft

Valenciana, Guanajuato

(Above) *Querétaro, Querétaro*

Crested grating of forged iron of colonial era.

(Left) *Puebla, Puebla*

Wrought iron at transom in old patio.

Near *Querétaro, Querétaro*

The Mudéjar geometric patterns of the *muntins* give an airy charm to the French-style windows of this isolated hacienda. However, it is probable that the panels now of glass were originally of wood and replaced at a later date.

Valenciana, Guanajuato

A skillfully fashioned stone corbel of rosy cast carries the projecting grillwork and creates the effect of an important oriel window.

Cuernavaca, Morelos

Dutch-style shutters in a remodeled colonial home. Installed in the same room as the earlier doors shown on page 98, they follow the latter in profile of panel moldings.

Tzintzuntzan, Michoacán

An early Franciscan monastery in the former capital of the Tarascan Indian kingdom known as "The Place of the Humming Birds."

Pátzcuaro, Michoacán

Where wood was available, hewn lintels were originally used.

Taxco, Guerrero

Thick exterior walls allow for recessed steps used when operating shutters and to reach the small seats on both sides of the window.

Taxco, Guerrero

The garden entrance to the Casa del Corazón, described by Anita Brenner in *Your Mexican Holiday* as "one of the loveliest houses in Taxco."

During its reconstruction, starting in 1928, for Señor don Moises Saenz, the architect, William Spratling, newly arrived from Tulane University and who later revived silver-smithing in Mexico, wrote and illustrated his book *Little Mexico*.

Alongside the portal at the head of a long and steep ramp is a masonry seat, called a "Beggars' Bench," where those seeking alms rested for expected gifts of coppers. The basic color of this joyously weatherworn garden wall is an intense blue, the masonry bench a Pompeian red and its wooden doors stained a blackish brown.

Taxco, Guerrero

The key escutcheon of the doors on the facing page with its angelic mermaids and flaming heart. The drapery held by the mermaids carries the legend: *"Aquí la puerta es corazón siempre abierta,"* the literal translation of which is, "Here the door is a heart always open." Both the escutcheon and the four-piece boss on the opposite page were fashioned by the students of a trade school under the jurisdiction of Señor Saenz, then the Sub-Secretary of Education.

Huejotzingo, Puebla

Imaginative use of moldings applied in fanlike design on plank doors.

Pátzcuaro, Michoacán

In the mode of the *plateresco* period in Spain (16th and first half of 17th centuries) is the finely scaled decoration of this carved stone hospital doorhead. The term *plateresco* designates ornament in the minute manner of the *plateros*, or silversmith's art. The later addition of out-of-scale lanterns was unfortunate.

(Above, left) *Morelia, Michoacán*

An entrance-door leaf from mid-18th century.

(Above, center) *Yuriria, Guanajuato*

One half of a *convento* doorway in *plateresco* style, about 1550.

(Above, right) *Cuernavaca, Morelos*

Small geometric paneling in deep reveal.

(Right) *Cuernavaca, Morelos*

Finely wrought ironwork on an old chest carved in shallow relief.

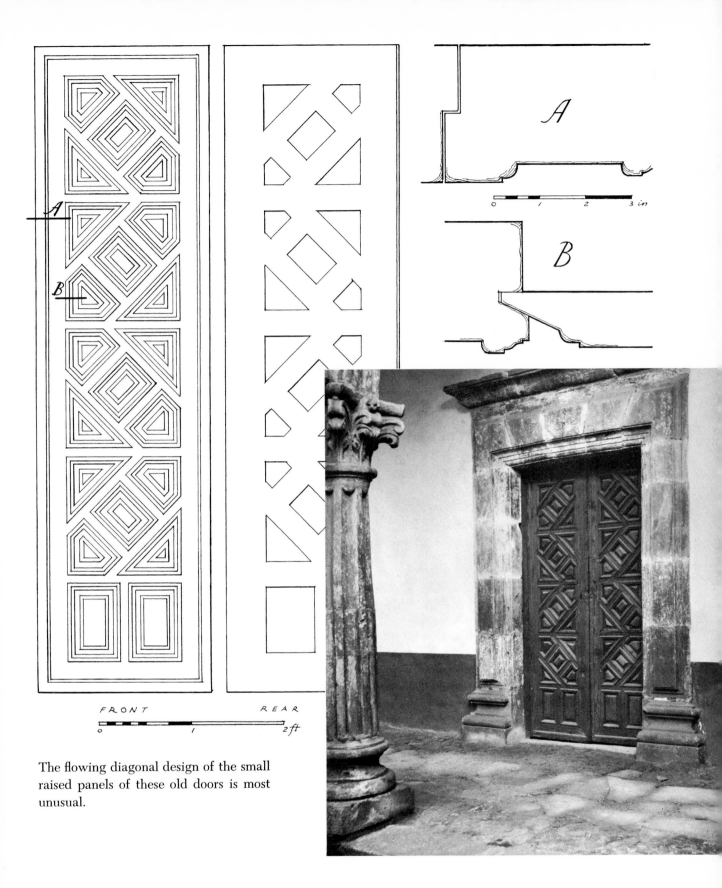

FRONT REAR

0   1   2 ft

The flowing diagonal design of the small
raised panels of these old doors is most
unusual.

Pátzcuaro, Michoacán

Marfil, Guanajuato

(Above) The impressive entrance to a *sala*. Lower half of one leaf of the heavy doors is separately hinged for easy access.

(Right) A unique interior shell head resulted from the undirected work of the maestro.

Marfil, Guanajuato

A primitive conception of the "Tree of Life," delicately carved in stone, enriches the pilasters and arched head of this minor entrance. It came originally from an Indian chapel of the early 18th century in northern Guanajuato. The carving just above the bases on both sides of the doorway is quite noticeably lower in relief than above, owing to continued rubbing by herds of goats.

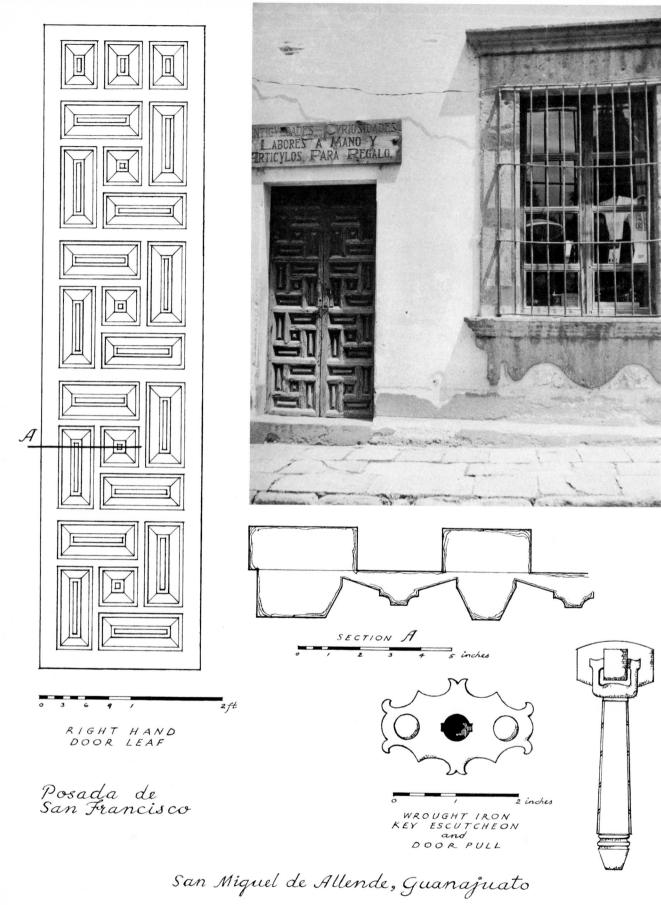

A

RIGHT HAND
DOOR LEAF

Posada de
San Francisco

SECTION A

0   1   2   3   4   5 inches

0   1   2 inches

WROUGHT IRON
KEY ESCUTCHEON
and
DOOR PULL

San Miguel de Allende, Guanajuato

Atotonilco, Guanajuato

Deep and bold reveals are characteristic of the early doors of Mexico.

(Above) *Guanajuato, Guanajuato*   (Below) *Querétaro, Querétaro*

Bizarre satyrs' faces and Moors' heads, known as *mascarones*, predominate in cast-iron and brass knockers on colonial doors.

Guanajuato, Guanajuato

These double doors, handsomely paneled and nail-studded, were moved from their
original position on an adjacent wall of the same house.

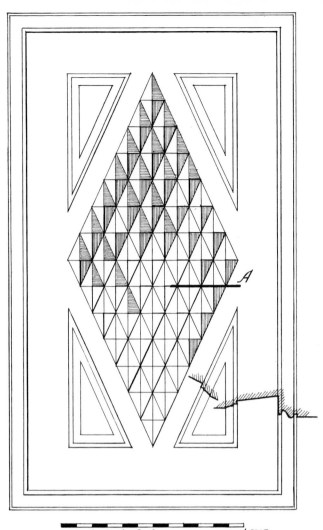

Cuernavaca , Morelos

Unique use of a conventionalized pineapple motif on a door panel.

The flat, metal-sheathed wood door is a heritage from the Moors. Here the ornamentation is formed with stapled wire.

Oaxaca , Oaxaca

A

Scale of Door
Scale of Details

0 3 6 9 1 2ft

0 1 2 3 4 5 6in

BRASS STRAP

Iglesia de Nᵃ Sᵃ de la Salud

San Miguel de Allende, Guanajuato

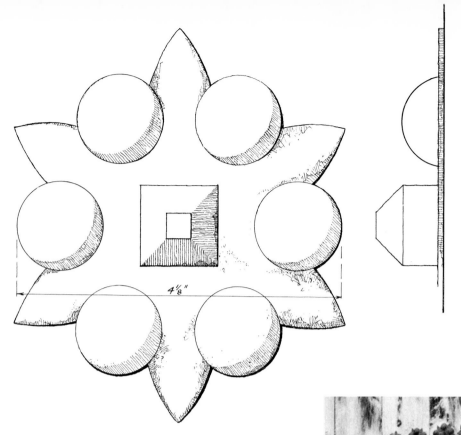

Yanhuitlán, Oaxaca

A door of a 16th-century Dominican monastery with wrought-iron nail heads ingeniously bossed.

Stout vertical boarding which presented entire exterior surface of door for iron decoration was of Moorish type.

Oaxaca, Oaxaca   *Querétaro, Querétaro*

The imagination used in the design of *mascarones* seems to be unlimited.

Oaxaca, Oaxaca

As the size and ornamentation of the nailhead grew, the nail was made separately and the decorative surround, either wrought or cast, became a large boss.

Querétaro, Querétaro

A pleasing effect produced with machines.

In wooded localities, open jig-sawn transoms are quite usual over 19th-century doorways. Both the wood members and surrounds in molded plaster are painted a soft, warm grey against walls of cream.

San Miguel de Allende, Guanajuato

From the early days of the 18th century, these doors have opened on the arcade,
bordering the plaza, of the former home of Don Manuel Tomás de la Canal.

Querétaro, Querétaro

(Above) Doorway at head of stairs on *galería* on page 35.

(Right) Under the exuberance of a baroque-headed arch-way was later added an iron grille of delightful design but of restrained classical forms reminiscent of the Adam brothers of England.

Querétaro, Querétaro

Rich in Churrigueresque motifs is the interior of the Church of Santa Clara. The sacristy door above is magnificent both in its capricious scrolling and its vigorous coloring. The carved relief is painted red, emphasized by bands and swirls of gold upon an olive-green background.

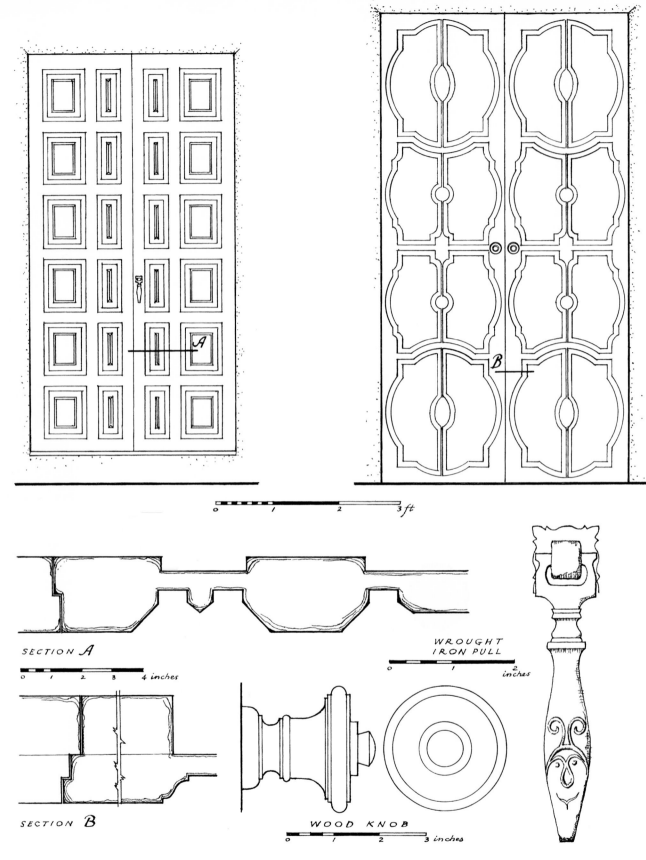

SECTION *A*

SECTION *B*

WROUGHT
IRON PULL

WOOD KNOB

Cuernavaca, Morelos

Cuernavaca, Morelos

Mexican doors are not only functional but, because of their paneling, serve as focal points in otherwise plain walls. Those above and as detailed on the opposite page are products of the 18th century.

The pair on the left, with their heavily raised panels and a wrought-iron pull, delicately embossed, was purchased in the 1940's at a demolition sale for 10 pesos. The pair on the right is unique in design. They were formerly in one of the homes of the Marquesa del Apartado.

(Above) *Morelia, Michoacán*

Typical of the Mexican colonial house is a large openwork gate or doorway separating the patio from the *zaguán,* an open passage from patio to street. Since the great doors of the *zaguán* stand open during the day, the pierced gate, called *portón* or *cancela,* partially screens the intimate patio from passers-by.

Morelia abounds in elaborate jig-sawn *cancelas* of the 19th century.

(Right) *Querétaro, Querétaro*
Machine-turned spindles and jig-sawn motifs appear oddly harmonious with a hand-shaped stone archway of a previous century.

Scale in inches

2 ¹³/₁₆"   1 ⁹/₁₆"

A   B

A JIGSAWN WOOD DOOR OF
INTRICATE DESIGN

Cuernavaca, Morelos

Guanajuato, Guanajuato

A monumental 18th-century *cancela*.

Pátzcuaro, Michoacán

Radiating wood spindles form a striking design for the *cancela* of this old convent.

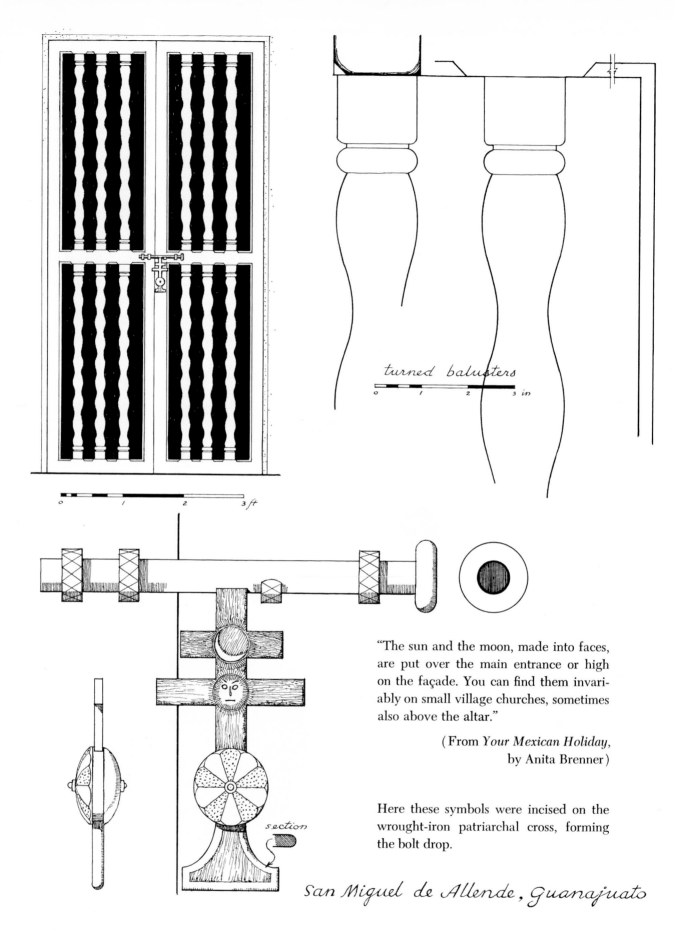

turned balusters

0   1   2   3 in

"The sun and the moon, made into faces, are put over the main entrance or high on the façade. You can find them invariably on small village churches, sometimes also above the altar."

(From *Your Mexican Holiday*, by Anita Brenner)

Here these symbols were incised on the wrought-iron patriarchal cross, forming the bolt drop.

section

San Miguel de Allende, Guanajuato

0   1   2   3 ft

San Miguel de Allende, Guanajuato

The polychrome arabesque, as developed by the Moors, ornaments the plastered dado, the door surround, and interior corners of the chapel at Instituto Allende. Baluster grilles forming the door, as detailed on the opposite page, give onto a small circular stone stairway leading to the roof.

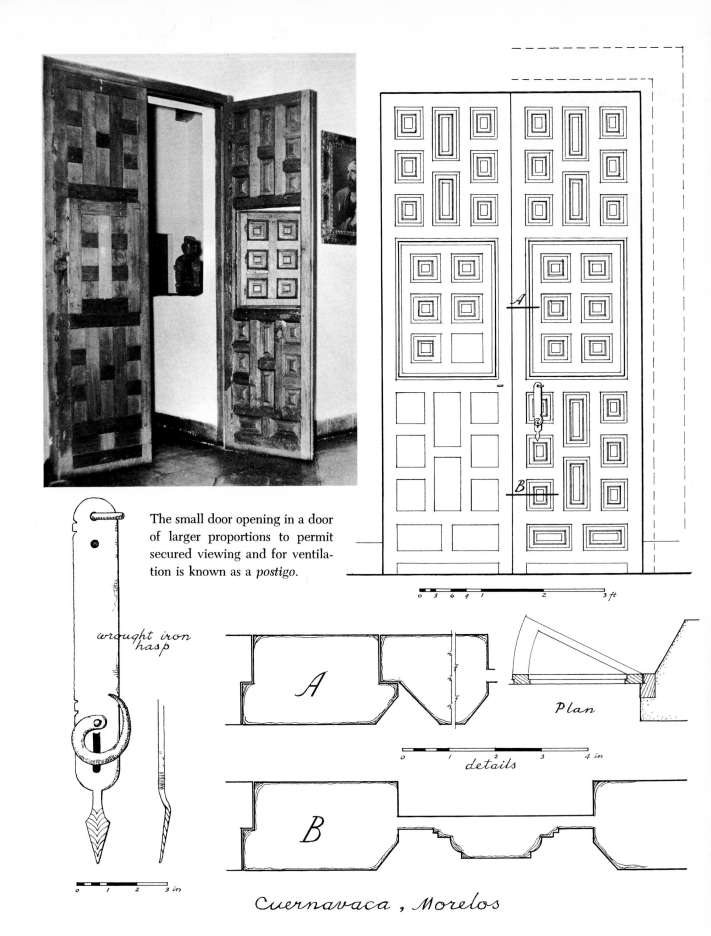

The small door opening in a door of larger proportions to permit secured viewing and for ventilation is known as a *postigo*.

wrought iron hasp

A

B

Plan

details

Cuernavaca, Morelos

(Above) *Cuernavaca, Morelos*

An arch-headed recess lined with glazed Puebla tiles, in blues, white, and yellows, set into a wall of soft cream, becomes a sort of quilted frame around a patio view.

(Left) *Querétero, Querétero*

Stone treads with wavelike outlines above polychromed tile risers.

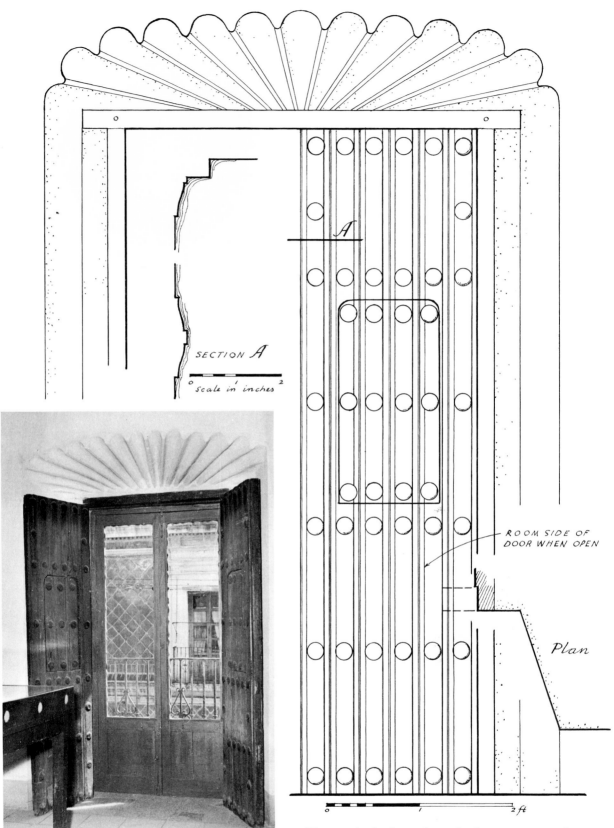

SECTION *A*

0   1   2
scale in inches

ROOM SIDE OF
DOOR WHEN OPEN

Plan

0   1   2 ft

Puebla , Puebla

Heavy plank shutters, with their *postigos*, close
this shell-headed, deeply recessed opening.

Puebla, Puebla

Over recessed doors and windows the local artisans shaped in plaster the concave side of a shell, known as a *concha*. Some were naturalistic, others conventionalized as in the example above from the *sacristía* of Casa del Alfeñique, or "Sugar-Cake House," of the late 17th century. Walls are white, painted decoration is pale blue, with window shutters in Chinese red and wainscot tile in yellows and greens on a white field.

Cuernavaca, Morelos

(Above) Doorway to kitchen as seen from extension of the *sala*.

(Right) Niche at dining area opening into *sala*. Masonry wall, with small pieces of stone pushed into mortar joints, are dark grey and waxed.

Cuernavaca, Morelos

Interior view of entranceway from *galería*, shown on page 14, into *sala*. The same shell contour is repeated over the deep splays opposite, producing an effect of decorative serenity. Against off-white walls the Pompeian red of the *concha*-headed recesses is imposing. (During the Crusades, a scallop or clam shell identified the carrier as a Christian pilgrim.)

(Upper left) An up-to-date home, no doubt through custom, uses the honored shell form of colonial Mexico.

(Upper right) Frequently, a niche in a stair wall will house the treasured statue of a saint.

(Below) In the lofty kitchen of an elaborate 18th-century manor house is this basin, originally containing water for cooking.

(Right) *Apaseo el Grande, Guanajuato*

Baroque *concha*, capricious in outline, in a manor house.

(Lower left) *Cuernavaca, Morelos*

Newly built but faithfully following an old motif.

(Lower right) *Apaseo el Grande, Guanajuato*

Francisco Tresguerras (1765-1863), said to be the last celebrated architect of the colonial period, introduced these unique *conchas* at four corners of a stair tower in a *convento*.

Apaseo el Grande, Guanajuato

The reverse side of doorway leading from the *galería* on page 2 to the rear roofs.

Candle-bearing wall brackets with elaborately tooled and embossed backplates of tin.

(Left) *Taxco, Guerrero*

Designed by David Adler, Architect

(Right) *Pátzcuaro, Michoacán*

The double-headed Hapsburg eagle, adopted by the Huichol Indians of Nayarit as a part of their mythology, crowns this wall lantern.

(Above) *Puebla, Puebla*

The open *galería* of La Casa del Alfeñique, of the late 17th century.

(Right) *Cuernavaca, Morelos*

Example of tin craftsmanship of today.

(Above) Chandelier of tin in the Museo de Tlaquepaque, Jalisco.

(Left) An arresting treatment of ironwork in Cuernavaca, Morelos.

A

B

C

D

Bracketed Lanterns:

a. Cuernavaca, Morelos
b. San Miguel de Allende, Guanajuato
c. Cuernavaca, Morelos
d. San Miguel de Allende, Guanajuato

Cuernavaca, Morelos

In area of continued moderate temperatures, outdoor living is at its best.
Across the patio from the loggia and over a swimming pool of lily-pad outline, you
look into a small *cantina,* or taproom, colorfully furnished with examples of native
crafts.

Cuernavaca, Morelos

(Above) Overlooking a view of rooftops eastward toward the mountains, the second-story loggia is well sheltered with southerly fold-back doors and canvas curtains. It is reached only by a stairway from the inner court below, a room apart, of complete privacy.

(Right) In the loggia entry, Santiago, patron saint of Spain, is carved in wood as a Crusader.

Cuernavaca, Morelos

(Above) For outdoor-indoor living, this sheltered extension of the garden is arranged with a satisfying mixture of informality and dignity.

(Left) Pink wall, white ceiling, a refectory table, with garden and sky included make up the charm of this dining area. A well-designed masonry settee forming a part of the wall lends repose and scale.

Cuernavaca, Morelos

Although the narrow strip of lawn between dining room and garden wall is only about six feet, the picture framed by the opened room end seems to recede into perspective and the small room stretches out to meet the wall — a veritable *trompe l'oeil*.

Cuernavaca, Morelos

(Left) Tucked into an interior angle of the loggia shown above is an intimate corner arranged around a built-in masonry seat. Colors reflect those of the wrapped-around garden. Plastered walls, white; seat pad, navy blue, with cushions striped in blue, grey and Nile green.

(Above) The soft hues of old quarry tile, hexagonal in form, pave the loggia of this modern home. Stone columns also are old, weathered, and charmingly out of line.

OPEN-WALLED ROOMS　115

Cuernavaca, Morelos

Into the freshness of today's Mexican homes are intimately blended treasures of the colonial era. Here a partially recessed cabinet of gilded wood with the patina of years projects from the wall above a sunken planting bed. Indirect lighting within the case accents its fascination.

Cuernavaca, Morelos

Charming view from *sala* is framed by deeply stained wood beams and stone columns of pinkish cast. The wide jambs of Pompeian red surrounded by off-white walls dramatize this composition.

Cuernavaca, Morelos

Our Lady of Guadalupe, or La Virgen de Tepeyac, patron saint of the Americas, serenely presides over the entryway of this remodeled colonial home.

Cuernavaca, Morelos

Scrolled and serpentine curves are applied in gesso to an old wood panel, five and one half feet high. Paneled moldings of the cupboard doors are touched with gold on a background of bottle green, complementing the greyed Pompeian red of the surrounding flat panel. The framing mold and appliquéd decorative motifs are gilded.

Cuernavaca, Morelos

A heavy, hewn-wood lintel supports a masonry hood on which the designer reproduced a 12th-century French fresco.

Near *Taxco, Guerrero*

A massive stone fireplace in a reconstructed-silver-ore hacienda, San Francisco Cuadra, founded in 1540.

Cuernavaca, Morelos

Two small and charming bedroom fireplaces of marked simplicity. Although fairly new, they have the mellowness of age.

(Above) *Cuernavaca, Morelos*

A modern fantasy. Inherited is the softly swaying outline of the hood of the chimney piece, backed against a modern sheet of glass.

(Left) *Apaseo el Grande, Guanajuato*

The painted brick checkerboard pattern of this ceiling is quite uncommon. The feathered headdress of the keystone figure greatly antedates the building of this *casa* in the early 1800's.

FIREPLACES   125

Cuernavaca, Morelos

An adaptation of the early method used in the construction of fireplaces. Although the hood projects, the fireplace proper is recessed in the masonry wall. Of interest, decoratively, is the importance of *santos*, or small statues of saints, with their bright glass eyes. The figures are modeled in gesso on carved wood and then painted in gorgeous tones of many colors.

Cuernavaca, Morelos

Designed with finesse. The masonry wall forms the backing of the flue within the projecting hood. A raised hearth, either built up or freestanding, is customary. Stressing the lofty ceiling is the high-climbing philodendron.

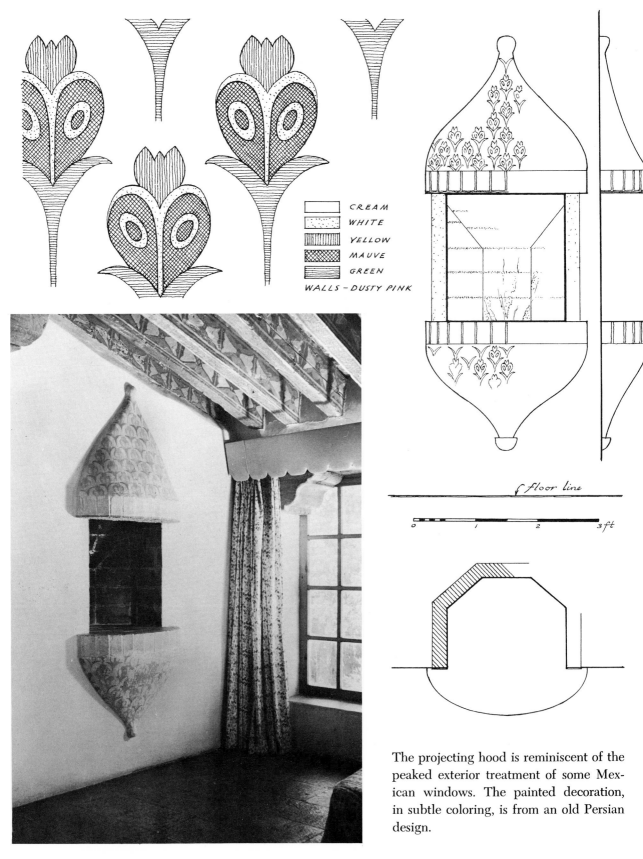

CREAM
WHITE
YELLOW
MAUVE
GREEN
WALLS – DUSTY PINK

floor line

0   1   2   3 ft

The projecting hood is reminiscent of the peaked exterior treatment of some Mexican windows. The painted decoration, in subtle coloring, is from an old Persian design.

Cuernavaca, Morelos

Corner fireplaces are of various forms, depending upon the whim of the designer.

(Above) *Morelia, Michoacán*

The beehive above is not only a source of heat for a bedroom, but also provides storage for a day's fuel under the cantilevered fireshelf.

(Left) *Cuernavaca, Morelos*

Conceived and executed by the local masonry maestro as proper for a small living room, the fireplace opposite has formal flanking piers.

Flagstone slabs form hearth, lintel, and flue, with the exterior masonry as backing for this small bedroom fireplace.

The metal chair in the foreground was designed by the owner.

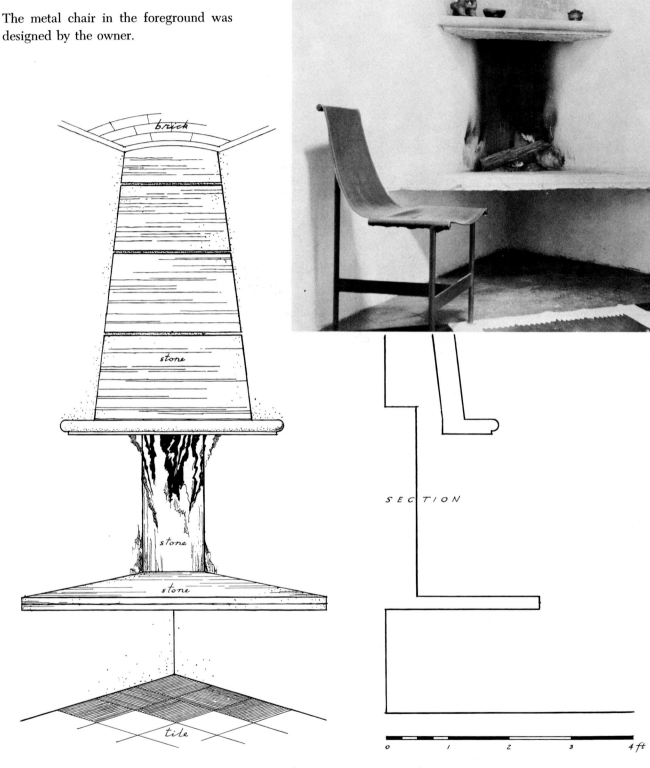

brick

stone

stone

stone

tile

SECTION

0   1   2   3   4 ft

Marfil, Guanajuato

Cuernavaca, Morelos

OUTDOOR FIREPLACE
Mexican in its details, this massive fireplace, which can also be used for barbecuing, is conveniently placed near the *cantina* and pool.

Apaseo el Grande, Guanajuato

The main *sala* of this fabulously ornate mansion is currently the storeroom for wood crates used in shipping the purple garlic which has been the principal product of this hacienda since its inception. The multicolored floral design completely covers the ceiling, giving the effect of small-patterned chintz. The elaborate *concha*, with angel below a plumed mask, crowns the doorway shown on page 33.

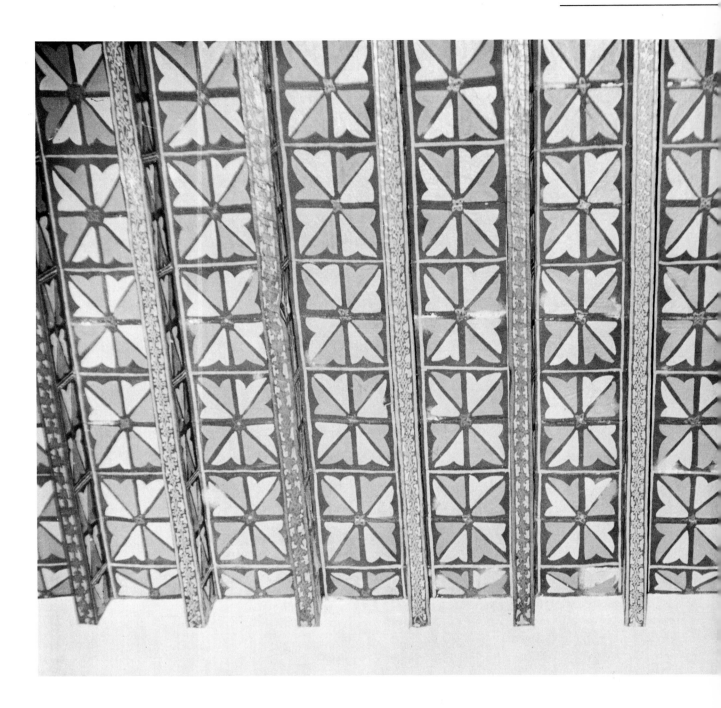

Cuernavaca, Morelos

Exposed tiles between wood beams are painted in geometric motifs of yellow and olive green upon a dark-green field. A touch of red accents the center of each squared rosette. The same design is repeated on the beam sides. A running pattern covers the soffits of the beams, alternating with red on light green, then orange and blue on green.

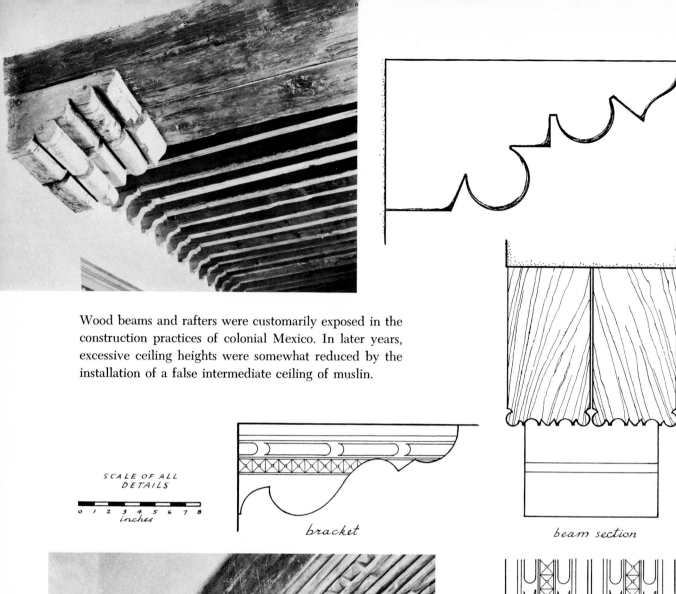

Wood beams and rafters were customarily exposed in the construction practices of colonial Mexico. In later years, excessive ceiling heights were somewhat reduced by the installation of a false intermediate ceiling of muslin.

SCALE OF ALL DETAILS

0 1 2 3 4 5 6 7 8
inches

bracket

beam section

beam soffit

Fluted and carved beams from an old Puebla building are here doubled to make a girder of imposing proportions.

Cuernavaca, Morelos

Morelia, Michoacán

In wooded regions around Morelia and Lake Pátzcuaro, ceiling beams were often spanned with boards instead of tile. At times thin hand-splits, called *tejamaniles,* were laid in herringbone pattern across the ceiling.

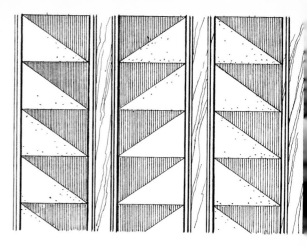

(Above) A 17th-century ceiling of the Casa de Alfeñique in Puebla inspired the brick decoration opposite. Mahogany-stained beams with molded soffits striped with gold leaf carry the reddish brown and white painted brick.

(Left) The ceilings of corridors and entryways are now and then barreled. Here the brick, painted blue and white, is supported by wood beams.

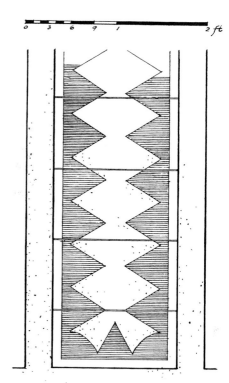

(Lower left & detail above) Light peach-colored beams form long ceiling panels of the same color bordered by triangles, like alligator teeth, in a darker tone.

Cuernavaca , Morelos

The bricks, spanning the beams to form the ceiling opposite, are colorfully decorated with painted squares in green on an off-white field. The soffits of the unfinished hewn beams are enriched with alternating geometric motifs in green and white.

Below is shown a modern version of the original technique. Here glazed tiles cemented to reinforced concrete above replace the painted brick. The triangular pattern in blue and white is laid to form squares, with blue-colored jointing cement where blue adjoins blue.

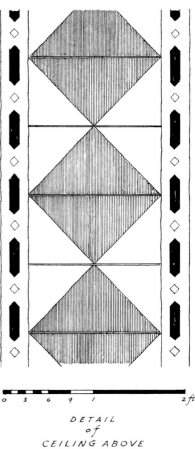

DETAIL
of
CEILING ABOVE

Cuernavaca , Morelos

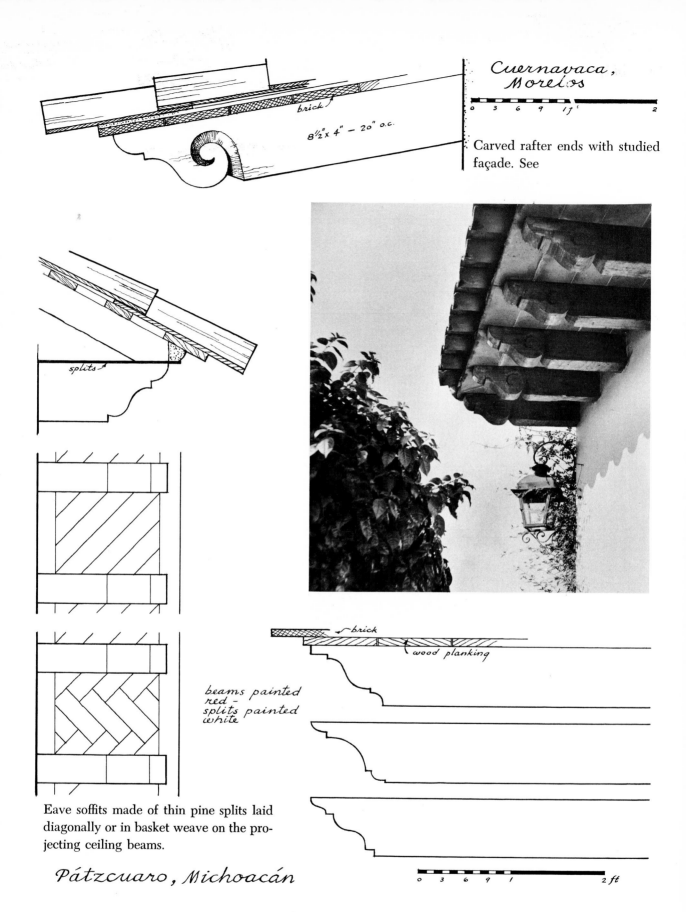

brick

$8\frac{1}{2}" \times 4" - 20"$ o.c.

Cuernavaca, Morelos

0 3 6 9 1' 2

Carved rafter ends with studied façade. See

splits

beams painted red - splits painted white

brick

wood planking

0 3 6 9 1' 2 ft

Eave soffits made of thin pine splits laid diagonally or in basket weave on the projecting ceiling beams.

Pátzcuaro, Michoacán

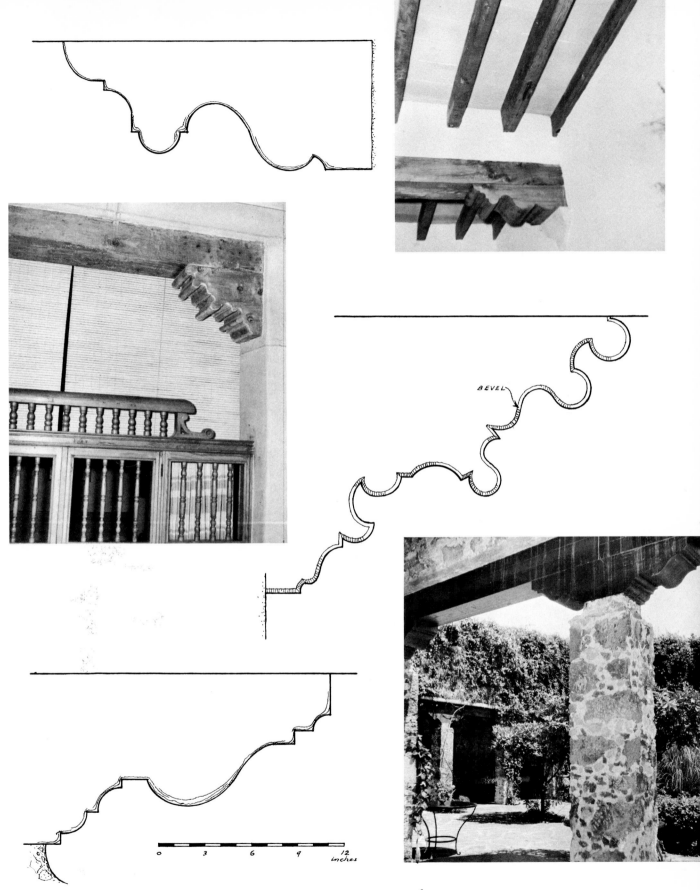

BEVEL

Cuernavaca, Morelos

(Above) *Pátzcuaro, Michoacán*

Wall design of doves with wreath, worked out in small glazed pottery jugs.

(Right) *Apaseo el Grande, Guanajuato*

Original masonry hood covered with reeded plaster above reconstructed *brasero*. The hood is vented through the chimney on page 13.

PHOTOGRAPH BY HUGO BREHME

(Above) *Puebla, Puebla*

17th-century kitchen. "We visited several Indian cottages, all clean and the walls hung with fresh mats, the floors covered with the same, and all with their kitchen utensils of baked earth neatly hung on the wall, from the largest size in use to little dishes and *jarritos* in miniature, which are only placed there for ornament."

Letter of 1841, from *Life in Mexico*.

(Left) *Cuernavaca, Morelos*

A modern adaptation. The kitchen walls are covered with glazed tiles of light beige, matching the color of the pottery.

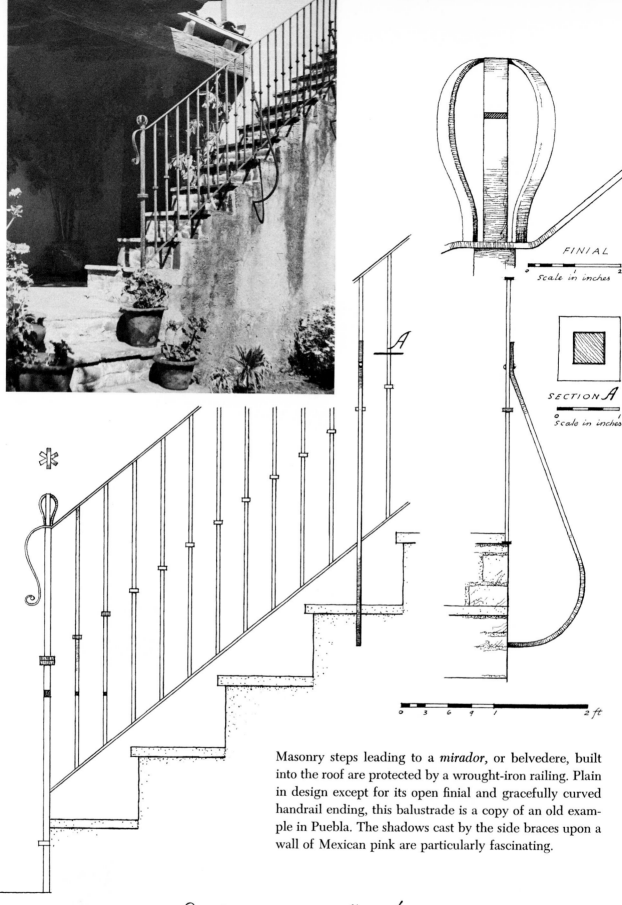

FINIAL

scale in inches

SECTION A

scale in inches

0 3 6 9 1   2 ft

Masonry steps leading to a *mirador,* or belvedere, built
into the roof are protected by a wrought-iron railing. Plain
in design except for its open finial and gracefully curved
handrail ending, this balustrade is a copy of an old example in Puebla. The shadows cast by the side braces upon a
wall of Mexican pink are particularly fascinating.

Cuernavaca , Morelos

(Above) *Tucson, Arizona*

Narrow stairs behind a stepped wall, framed by a patio archway, recall the craftsmanship of colonial Mexico. Built in 1937, this house follows conventions of the period when this region was a part of the Spanish Empire. Walls of the patio are off-white in tone, with paving of pink Arizona flagging.

(Right) *Marfil, Guanajuato*

Steps for men and a ramp for burros leading to an elevated tank room over the cisterns. The checkerboard paving of the court is of greenish cast, while the masonry walls of the inclined passageway are peach in color.

A decorative wood guard rail protects a ramp, used by
burros and men, leading to the *galería* of one of the many
patios of El Convento de los Once Patiòs.

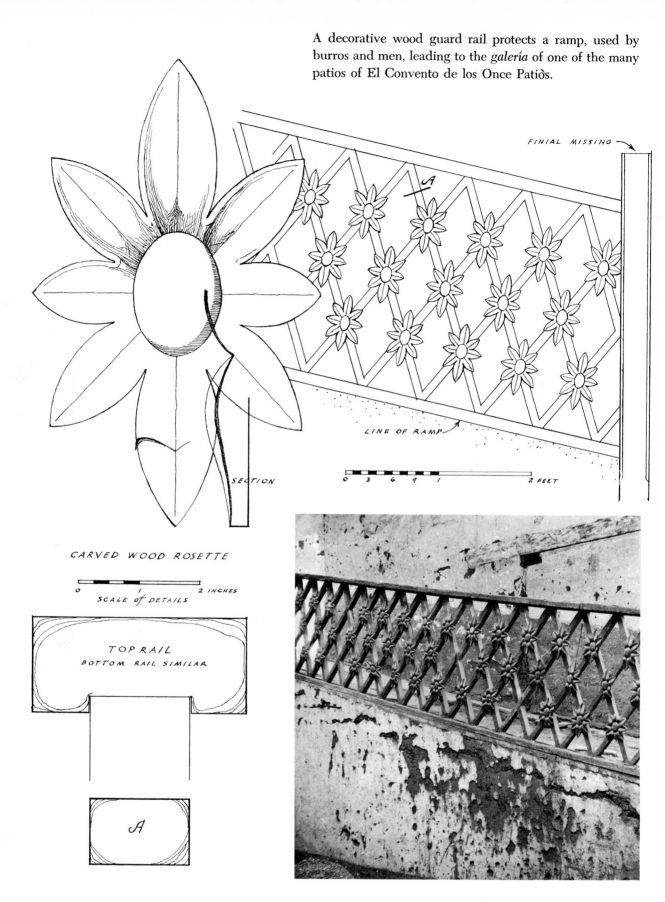

FINIAL MISSING

A

LINE OF RAMP

0 3 6 9 1 2 FEET

SECTION

CARVED WOOD ROSETTE

0 1 2 INCHES
SCALE of DETAILS

TOP RAIL
BOTTOM RAIL SIMILAR

A

Pátzcuaro, Michoacán

Cuernavaca, Morelos

Actually a new house built old. Collected by the owner were fragments and bits such as the blue-and-white glazed tiles, *azulejos*, at the stair.

(Above) *Puebla, Puebla*

Two views of patio stairway in Casa del Alfeñique. With a robust twist, the bold stone handrail ends against a small realistic lion.

(Right) *Pátzcuaro, Michoacán*

Expertly stylized lion forming the newel head in an old house.

Valenciana, Guanajuato

A quaint wooden stairway winds up to a door, high in the wall, giving onto additional steps of masonry to the *azotea,* a flat roof serving many purposes.

San Miguel de Allende, Guanajuato

Inviting flight of steps leading to a guest-house terrace. Fine glazed tiles surface the risers in tier upon tier of pattern.

Cuernavaca, Morelos

An old carved-stone animal figure forms the newel head for this exterior stairway
with its heavy stone treads and risers of blue-and-white tile, all against walls of pale
Mexican pink.

A B

a, b, & c. *San Miguel de Allende, Guanajuato.* Imaginative caps from small flues.
d. *Marfil, Guanajuato.* The massive top of an old furnace.

C

Cuernavaca, Morelos

Chimney cappings play a decorative part in the skyline of Cuernavaca.

The octagonal cap crowned with tile (*above*) is similar to those of the Island of Majorca.

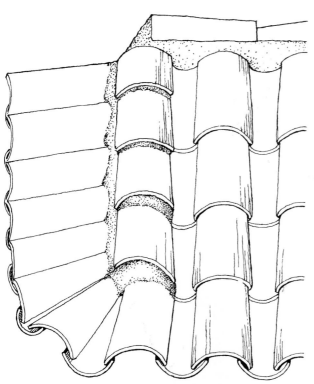

COPING COURSE ABOUT 2½"
HIGHER THAN FIELD COURSES

Tehuantepec, Oaxaca

San Jacinto, Oaxaca

Without a weatherproof coping, an adobe wall disintegrates rapidly. The projecting roofing tiles provide this cover, like a ruffled headdress.

*near
Oaxaca, Oaxaca*

B

Cuernavaca, Morelos

a & b. Wood rafters support wide, thin brick surfaced with cement and a membrane waterproofing on which the pan and cover tile are laid.

c, d, & e. Interesting treatments of eave and rakes. Masonry cornice with corbeled roofing tile. Small holes in the cement fill at eaves provide ventilation.

D

E

San Miguel de Allende, Guanajuato
Patio in the Instituto Allende.

"A Mexican patio, in fact, is considerably more than a courtyard. It is a flower garden surrounded by a house."

from *Viva Mexico!*
by Charles Macomb Flandrau

(Above) *Valenciana, Guanajuato*

Heavily weathered stone wellhead, surmounted
by a finely wrought-iron pulley standard, in the
sun-drenched cloister of the great church of San
Cayetano, dedicated in 1788 and built by the
Conde Rul.

(Left) *Puebla, Puebla*

Stone *mascarón*, or decorative mask, whose mouth
forms a water spout, built into the wall of an inner
court.

(Above) *Cuernavaca, Morelos*

A cleverly composed bedroom terrace abutting the property wall, all in deep Mexican pink, overlooks a raised garden pool.

(Left) *Pátzcuaro, Michoacán*

A sunken bath pool in the former Convento de Once Patios. Water, both hot and cold, from cisterns in the adjoining room flowed into the bath through the stone masks.

(Above) *Cuernavaca, Morelos*

Tiled pool in an inner court, where the low Romanesque-like arches were raised upon foundations put in place by a lieutenant of Cortés in the mid-16th century.

(Left) Near *Guanajuato, Guanajuato*

Cut-stone wall fountain with pleasing curves.

Cuernavaca, Morelos

(Above) In a walled garden, running parallel with an outdoor-indoor *corredor*, gurgles a delicate jet of water rising from a rectangular pool and surrounded by a collection of flower pots secured from old haciendas where they were originally used in the processing of sugar cane.

(Right) Originals or replicas of pre-Conquest gods, carved from lava rock, are effectively placed overlooking garden areas. Because of its turban, this figure is thought to represent an Oaxaca deity of lower-middle culture.

(Above) *Cuernavaca, Morelos*

Carved stone font with circular stone seat at end of garden entrance steps. Recently built around colonial motifs.

(Right) *San Miguel de Allende, Guanajuato*

Patio fountain of an old colonial town house. Glazed tiles were frequently used for both exterior surfacing and interior linings.

Cuernavaca, Morelos

A shallow reflecting pool, open to the sky, forms an extension to this impressive loggia. Over the rim of the shell-shaped wall basin trickles a curtain of water. The motar joints of the buff-grey stonework are chinked with a lacelike tracery of small chips of roofing tile, recalling the pinkish grey of the columns. This color is repeated in the tile *citarillas* with their alternating rows of interstices filled with a light-cream mortar.

Cuernavaca, Morelos

Luxuriant in design and in tropical foliage, this *mise-en-scène*, viewed through a glass wall, creates an illusion of greater width to the *sala*.

Cuernavaca, Morelos

Below the living-room terrace, a small swimming pool occupies with grace and charm the lower level of a confined city site.

Cuernavaca, Morelos

A plastered masonry shell forms a delightful background for a small pool in the corner of an intimate garden.

Cuernavaca, Morelos

A charming asset handed down from the Moors was the skillful use of water in pictorial effects.

(Above) From a little jet rising and falling alongside the stone dog, poised on top of an old column capital, water trickles into the pool. Then the water slowly overflows into a channel under the flagging leading to the canal opposite.

(Right) A flower-edged canal, fed by the fountain, seems to glide the length of the garden.

(Above) *Marfil, Guanajuato*

Surrounded by potted white geraniums, a sunbleached wooden *santa* completes a terrace vista.

(Right) *Cuernavaca, Morelos*

Curved to retain, at a higher level, the roots of a spreading tree, this masonry wall with its evenly spaced row of sugar pots is completely covered with the closely clinging fig vine, called *monedita*.

Cuernavaca, Morelos

Plastered masonry benches built against walls are architectural features of many gardens.

(Right, above) Pineapple finial for clothes pole made from band and sheet iron.

The Mexican choice of garden sculpture is extremely varied, from pre-Conquest gods such as that shown on page 158 to the bibulous lady and angel below, and the *mamacita*, or little mother, right. The latter, immediately inside the entrance shown on page 70, sits serenely overlooking a small pool.

(Left) Near *San Juan del Rio, Querétaro*

(Left, below) Near *Yautepec, Morelos*

(Right, below) *Apaseo el Grande, Guanajuato*

The curves of the gateway head and parapet walls follow the flowing lines of the baroque.

Cuernavaca, Morelos

A distinguished walled gateway forms the main entrance to a recently built country estate. Chips of terra-cotta-colored tile inserted into the mortar joints of the lava rock weave a colorful pattern.

Cuernavaca, Morelos

(Left) A miniature colonnade of plastered masonry with brick capitals and coping and arches formed with roofing tile.

(Below) Pierced wall of shaped brick adds privacy to this garden retreat at the base of a very old tree.

San Miguel de Allende,
Guanajuato

For both the wall above, festooned with geraniums, and that below, arched with clipped privet supported by steel rods, foliage forms an integral part of the design.

Cuernavaca, Morelos

Walls in Mexico, whether of buildings or fences, are for the most part of some form of masonry construction.

Here in these recently built walls, using the same thin brick, two distinctly different effects have been achieved, each to serve its own purpose.

(Left) With the brick laid on end, a louvered wall is produced which screens and yet allows the passage of air into a drying yard.

(Below) Again, with the brick laid on end but at right angles to the face, each opening has been filled with a brick alternating between the exterior and interior faces to form a solid wall enclosing a work yard. The sloping half-bricks in the recessed panels of the exterior face not only contribute to the feeling of solidity, but also provide surfaces for the changing shadows.

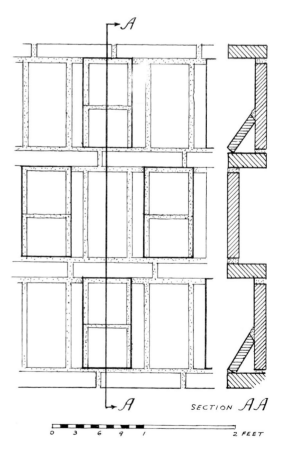

SECTION *AA*

0 3 6 9 1   2 FEET

San Miguel de Allende, Guanajuato

172 CITARILLAS

The *citarilla*, an open fence of balustrade usually built of shaped bricks or tile, is one of the most distinctive and most frequently seen features of the Mexican style of building.

(Above) Near *Tula, Hidalgo*

Fashioned by the repetition of cleverly designed mold topped by a rail edged with scallops, all of burned clay.

(Below) *Querétaro, Querétaro*

An effective lacelike *citarilla* made up of rectangles and half circles.

(Left) An open geometric pattern of brick dignified by plastered masonry columns encloses a part of the gardens. Built by José de la Borda in the 18th century. In 1864 these gardens became part of the summer home of Maximilian and Carlotta.

(Below) A more simple use of the design above.

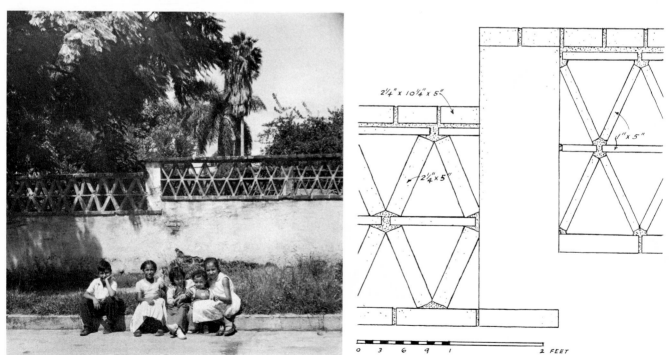

2¼" x 10¼" x 5"

2¼" x 5"

1" x 5"

0   3   6   9   1   2 FEET

Cuernavaca, Morelos

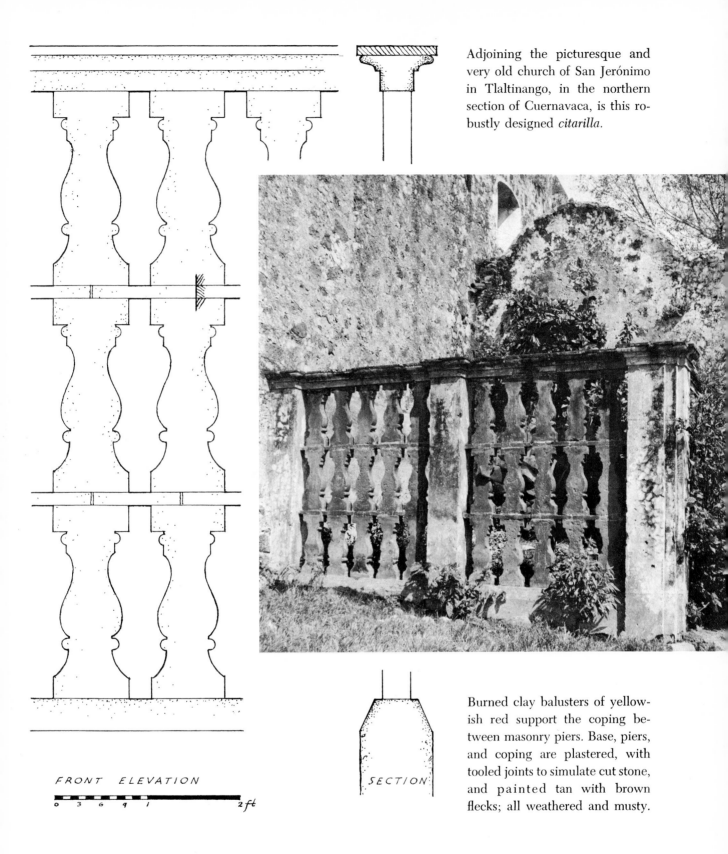

Adjoining the picturesque and very old church of San Jerónimo in Tlaltinango, in the northern section of Cuernavaca, is this robustly designed *citarilla*.

Burned clay balusters of yellowish red support the coping between masonry piers. Base, piers, and coping are plastered, with tooled joints to simulate cut stone, and painted tan with brown flecks; all weathered and musty.

FRONT ELEVATION

0 3 6 9 1   2 ft

SECTION

Cuernavaca, Morelos

Two open parapets, with plastered brick copings, made up of half circles of clay tile in varying combinations. By filling certain continuous or alternate rows of openings with mortar, diverse effects are achieved. An example of this diversity is the *citarilla* on page 160.

(Above) The Mexicans' inherent love of growing things changes a plain retaining wall into a floral display by the addition of tiers of masonry shelves to carry their potted plants.

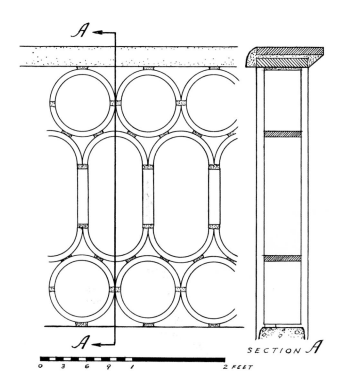

SECTION A

0 3 6 9 1   2 FEET

(Right) Open screenlike patterns allow for a dappled play of light and shadow.

Taxco, Guerrero

Cuernavaca, Morelos

(Above) Panels of white marble pieces bedded in light grey cement, and large brown pebbles laid in cement colored with a brush coat of brown earth, all outlined by red brick on edge, form the surface of this driveway.

(Right) Diagonal stripes of pieces of white marble and of black volcanic rock laid in grey cement.

PAVING

(Above) Panels of white marble pieces and brown pebbles, with brick dividers, surround this small patio fountain. (Below) Varied uses of the same materials to form contrasting patterns in driveway.

(Above) *Marfil, Guanajuato*

Rough rubble masonry using green-grey native limestone. Joints filled with lighter-colored chips of same material.

(Right) *Morelia, Michoacán*

Walls faced with pink and yellow weathered stone. Relatively tight joints are diagonally filled with splittings of the same material. Cut-stone window trim.

(Above) Near *Cuautla, Morelos*

Wall of hacienda church. Mixed masonry with fish-scale pattern of black stone chips embedded in plastered surface.

(Right) *Cuernavaca, Morelos*

Palacio de Cortés, built about 1531. Rubble masonry of volcanic rock, or *tezontle*, with large red pieces set in joints for weather protection of mortar.

Mexico City

The wall facing of the 18th-century mansion, Casa de los Azulejos, or House of Tiles. The façade was covered with blue-and-white Puebla tiles by the Condesa del Valle de Orizaba. This is said to be the finest secular example in Mexico of Mudéjar influence. Arabic motifs, possibly somewhat modified, are characteristic of the Mudéjar.

Puebla, Puebla

Puebla de los Angeles, or City of the Angels, established in 1532, became famous for its hand-wrought tile. These colorful *azulejos* were lavishly used not only in conventional ways for floors, walls, and ceilings, but became in many instances a distinguishing feature of exterior wall surfacing. Most frequently, blue-and-white glazed tiles were set into a ground of red brick.

Near *Real del Puente, Morelos*

A local grass, *sacate de casa*, lends itself to fine-textured thatching. This new home still carries its cross of benediction.

Matzatlán, Sinaloa

A palmetto-thatched shelter, known as a *ramada*, provides welcome shade from the midday sun.

East of Cordoba, Vera Cruz

Excessive rainfall requires a steeply pitched thatched roof. Openings in gable ends under the ridge provide ventilation.

(Above) *Huichiuayan, San Luis Potosí*

(Below) *Tamazunchale, San Luis Potosí*

Thatched with *sacate*, the local grass, with wide roof overhangs to protect the plastered adobe walls from the frequent rains.

(Above) *Real del Monte,*
near *Pachuca, Hidalgo*

A typical gable end of hand-split
shakes laid fanlike. The adobe
bricks below are of natural pinkish tan, with plastered wall under eaves painted a vivid blue.

(Below) Near *Las Vigas,*
Vera Cruz

In the higher mountain areas,
steeply pitched roofs are shin-
gled with long thin slats.

On road from *Cuernavaca* to *Yautepec, Morelos*

Thatch-roofed grain bins with plastered wattle walls, known as *cuezcomate,* are typical of this area.

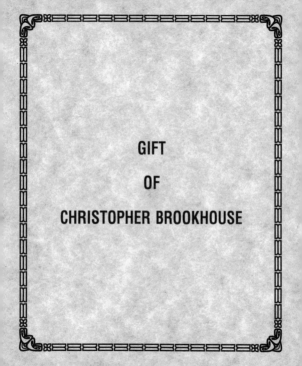